Psalms

© John Wright 2024

John Wright asserts his right to be identified as the creator of the design of the format of the contents contained within this work

This book is sold subject to the condition that the format within it shall not, by way of trade or otherwise, be copied unless the prior written consent of the author or any publisher to whom he delegates authority has been obtained, and without a similar condition including this condition being imposed on the subsequent purchaser

Designer: John E Wright

Contact: essbj@aol.com

The designer acknowledges the likelihood of errors and spelling mistakes, and will correct and republish speedily following any such discovery(ies)

Dedication

In 2004, Megan Sprinks died. Among her effects was a Holy Bible whose spine bore in filigree lettering the words 'NEW TRANSLATION'. Inscribed on a fly-leaf was the dedication "A recognition of a kindness and help received from her by *E E F Bush*

Megan Sprinks was my Mum's mother. The Bible was a translation of the Holy Scriptures by John Nelson Darby (one of the influential figures among the original Plymouth Brethren). It came into my possession and I prefer to read this version or sometimes the Authorised Version (King James Version "KJV")

This effort on the author's part, to modernise the language a little, is dedicated to both my Nana and my mum. Special thanks also to my mum who noticed errors which had escaped my eye.

And, as someone with faith in Jesus Christ (believing that he is the living Son of God, who shall one day come again to earth), I dedicate this 'effort' to Him and to the glory of God.

Introduction

For some time, I have pondered upon embarking on the significant undertaking of contemplating the version of the Holy Bible translated by John Nelson Darby ('Darby'), and tweaking the archaic language he adopted when he originally translated in the nineteenth century. He admits (in his own introduction) that the language he used in his translations of the Holy Scriptures was influenced by his intense usage of the KJV.

This offering is not a translation. It is definitely not a commentary. It is not a paraphrasing version. It is more a 'simple' review of the language Darby used and his frequent use of detailed footnotes. It provides the reader with a different layout of the Psalms (no columns) where the footnotes are less distracting compared to Darby's version.

I have tried to make any footnotes easier to cross-reference, generally limiting reference to them in most psalms with these symbols:

* ~ ^ + ^^ ** ~~ ++

For longer psalms where there are a multitude of footnotes, numbers are used in point size 9 (with any footnotes related to the psalm's header cross-referenced in symbols).

Occasionally, after the English translation I've placed the Hebrew word in brackets so that the reader can consider the particular meaning of the translation (e.g there are different words for 'man', 'people', 'earth',etc).

Thanks to Darby, I appreciate that there are a multitude of words which we read in various translations without realising that they might mean something different to what we expect when we are informed of how the word is and could be translated.

Being a songwriter and poet, my aim was to be sensitive in adjusting words, and so I have deliberately avoided some stylistic changes. For example, I have opted to leave alone 'terrible', meaning (as I believe) the ability to create or instil terror. Generaly I adopt the abbreviated form 'don't' for 'do not'. The archaic word 'lest' has been altered to "in case". 'Yea' is changed to 'yes'. 'Lo' and 'behold' and 'laud' are usually left unaltered; 'therein' and 'withal' have sometimes been altered.

In the current decade, the origin of words seems to have been discarded, so the reader is encouraged to think for themselves about what the words reveal in their context. We can access a dictionary where needed.

Darby's version of the Holy Scriptures, along with Young's, is credited as being a superior literal translation of the ancient texts (from which we have the holy scriptures) without veering towards any doctrinal bias. Simply put: you read, it's up to you to think over what you read, and to reach your own conclusion.

This is what Darby thought of the Holy Scriptures irrespective of his translation:

> "I believe the Scriptures to be the inspired word of God, received by the Holy Spirit and communicated by His power, though, thank God, through mortal man..."

I share Darby's conviction. I acknowledge all the hard work of translating should be credited to Darby and his original team. My contribution is to sensitively tweak the language to something closer to what we use in the twenty-first century. Darby's version appears to now be in the public domain, so there appears to be no copyright. However, if an entity comes forward claiming copyright, I am willing to have a discussion about this offering.

Before providing the 150 psalms, some explanatory definitions are included for words which frequently appear but have varying meanings depending on the Hebrew word. One example is 'people'.

Footnotes are given to help with words or phrases which might be translated in more than one way. Different 'special' characters are used to draw the reader's attention to alternative translations of a given word or phrase.

Where the reader sees a word or words in [ ] marks, to quote from Darby's own introduction to his translation: they "indicate (a) words added to complete the sense in English, (b) words as to which there are variations in the original manuscripts".

Wherever possible, each psalm begins on a new page with the exception of those psalms which are six to eight verses in length. The left hand and right hand margin of the page are wide, allowing the reader to make annotations.

Some observations

This publication is not a thesis on the nature of the psalms.

Readers may or not be aware that the Jewish king, David, is not the author of all the psalms.

Many psalms have no accredited author, as the reader will see.

The psalms comprise five books.

The content of some psalms can be found within other books of the Old Testament Scriptures (e.g. Samuel, Chronicles).

It is worth reading 1 Chronicles 15 and 16 because it makes sense of some of the words often displayed with the Psalm header (e.g Jeduthun, Sheminith etc – see notes in 'Words frequently occurring in the psalms etc'). It should also enlighten us with the relevance of 'to the chief Musician', often seen at the head of psalms, and clarify why 'the sons of Korah' and Asaph are referenced.

Some psalms (e.g 25,34,119) are acrostic with each verse or half-verse or stanza starting with the beginning letter of the Hebrew alphabet working through to the end of the Hebrew alphabet.

God is a personal God who has many names. Darby generally refers to Him personally as Jehovah or Jah ('the existing One' objectively), and less frequently as 'Lord' or 'God'. Adonai is usually translated 'God' in translations of scripture. Other names for God include Adonai Jehovah, or Jehovah Elohim, El Shaddai, Jehovah Jireh etc.

Selah frequently occurs in the book of psalms. Its meaning is not certain. It might be a pointer to take a pause. Some take it to mean a direction to the singers to raise their voices.

Higgaion appears in psalms 9 and 92: it may mean 'to be played on the harp' or a musical instrument; or, alternatively, 'meditate' (as in Psalm 19v14).

The Old Testament comprises 1131 chapters (thank you, monks). 150 psalms equates to 13+% of the chapters of the Old Testament.

Psalm 119

Known for being the longest 'chapter' in the Bible, comprising 176 verses.

It is an alphabetical psalm, comprising 22 stanzas of 8 verses. In the first stanza, each verse starts with the first letter of the Hebrew alphabet, Aleph. The second stanza is the same: each verse starts with the second letter, Beth, and so on throughout each stanza.

The word translated 'statutes' could read 'ordinances' throughout.

Darby's footnote for the word translated 'statutes' references Exodus 12 v24 (where the context is God's guidance to his people concerning keeping the passover, that it should be observed as an 'ordinance', the footnote by Darby there stating that the word is generally 'statute'). It occurs 22 times in the psalm.

There is a distinction between *dabar* and *imrah* throught the psalm.

dabar is 'word' and smilar to *'logos'* in the New Testament.

omer and *imrah* mean 'a word' or 'speech' or 'what is said', and usually employed in poetic style only (except Joshua 24 v27).

imrah is differentiated from *dabar* in the psalm simply: *imrah* is usually shown in brackets.

imrah is found in a feminine form in verse 11 only. Using 'word' in that verse instead of 'saying' appeared preferable to Darby because it fixes the mind on what is expressed.

Words occuring frequently in the psalms with various meanings

people
leummim races having a common origin – associated peoples. It's always plural in the psalms
ammim peoples viewed as of one kind or having one purpose (tribes or nations); for or against God and his people

man
enosh feeble, mortal man looked at as a race, in contrast with distinguished individuals
adam (or *Adam*) man or original man
geber in Job 3v3 and lots of psalms: it refers to strength, *gibbor* being used for 'mighty men' or 'heroes'

chasid and chesed
chasid adjective. Used for man and for God. Translated 'holy', 'pious', 'saint', 'gracious'
chesed noun. 'piety' and recognition of God on man's part; 'grace' and 'loving-kindness' on God's part

word
There are multiple Hebrew and Greek meanings for 'word' when we read 'word' in the scriptures.

dabar is similar to *logos* (Greek) in the New Testament. (See the preceding notes relating to Psalm 119)

wisdom
chakam "intelligence", "circumspection", "understanding"

fool
nabal "fool", "ungodly", "impious", "vile", or it can mean an empty person;
eveel is a generic word for 'fool' with two shades of meaning:
    it is opposite to *chakam* (wise) or *aroom* (prudent, wary);
    the idea of wickedness is not absent
kesil usually translated 'foolish'

Other words

erets 'land' or 'country', but with the plural 'ends of the earth' (Ps2) could mean 'earth'
tebel the habitable earth

Sheol 'Hades' – it vaguely expresses the place or state of the soul separated from the body

tzar the adversary of Christ, or oppressor of the remnant from within

oyeb external 'enemy' (in Psalms 8,18 etc)

workers the Hebrew word is used for folks who do 'mighty deeds', 'achievements', and is common throughout the psalms

temple the Hebrew word can often mean 'palace'

perversion 'the Hebrew word covers corrupt, depraved desires', 'wickedness', 'mischievous things. It's plural

Phrases at the start of some psalms

nehiloth (Ps5) 'pipes' or 'flutes' (wind instruments) – word derives from 'to pierce'

sheminith (Ps6) may mean 'on the octave' or 'with eight strings'

gittith (Ps8,81,84) a musical instrument, root word derived from 'vat' or 'press'

muthlabben (Ps9) may mean 'the death of [his] son'

michtam (Ps16,56-60) meaning 'golden'

aijeleth-shahar (Ps 22) means 'according to the hind of the morning'

jeduthun (Ps39,62,77) meaning 'praising' or 'celebrating'

shoshannim (Ps45,69,80) meaning 'lilies'

alamoth (Ps46) it's the plural of 'virgin', 'young women'; may mean 'for virgin voices'

mahalath (Ps53) means 'sickness'. The Hebrew word is aligned with 'sick'

mahalath leannoth (Ps88) – leannoth is probably the plural of 'wormwood'. The combined phrase may mean 'for pensive singing'

jonath-elem-rechokim (Ps56) is 'the mute dove in the distance'

shushan (Ps60) means 'lily'

Psalm 1

1 Blessed is the man that does not walk in the counsel of the wicked and does not stand in the way of sinners, and does not sit in the seat* of scorners;
2 but his delight is in Jehovah's law, and in his law he meditates day and night.
3 And he is~ as a tree planted by brooks of water, which gives its fruit in its season and whose leaf does not fade; and all that he does prospers.
4 The wicked are not so; but are as chaff which the wind drives away.
5 Therefore the wicked shall not stand in the judgment, nor sinners in the assembly of the righteous.
6 For Jehovah knows the way of the wicked shall perish.

*or 'in the company'   ~ or 'will be'

Psalm 2

1 Why are the nations in tumultuous agitation, and [why] do the peoples *(leummim)* meditate a vain thing?
2 The kings of the earth set themselves*, and the princes plot together, against Jehovah and against his anointed:
3 Let us break their bonds asunder and cast away their cords from us!
4 He that dwells in the heavens shall laugh, the Lord shall have them in derision.
5 Then he will speak to them in his anger, and in his fierce displeasure he will terrify them:
6 And I have anointed~ my king upon Zion, the hill of my holiness.
7 I will declare the decree: Jehovah has said to me,
"You are my Son, this day I have begotten you.
8 Ask of me, and I will give you nations for an inheritance, and for your possession the ends of the earth. *(erets)*
9 You shall break them with a sceptre^ of iron, as a potter's vessel you shall dash them in pieces."
10 And now, O kings, be wise+, be admonished, you judges of the earth.
11 Serve Jehovah with fear, and rejoice with trembling.
12 Kiss the Son, in case he be angry and you perish in the way, though his anger burns but a little^^. Blessed are all who have their trust** in him.

* or 'stand up'   ~ or 'installed'   ^ or 'rod'   + or 'consider well'   ^^ or 'for his anger soon burns'   ** or 'take refuge'. Same root word as 'refuge' in Ps 14v6 and 'trust' in 2 Samuel 22 v3

Psalm 3
A psalm of David, when he fled from Absalom, his son

1 Jehovah, how many are they that trouble* me, many that rise up against me!
2 Many say of my soul, "There is no salvation for him in God". Selah.
3 But you, Jehovah, are a shield about me: my glory, and the lifter up of my head.
4 With my voice I will call to Jehovah, and he will answer me from the hill of his holiness. Selah.
5 I laid down and slept; I awaked, for Jehovah sustains me.
6 I will not fear for myriads of the people that have set themselves against me round about.
7 Arise, Jehovah; save me, my God! For you have smitten all my enemies on the cheekbone, you have broken the teeth of the wicked.
8 Salvation is of Jehovah; your blessing is upon your people. Selah.

* hints at Tzar

Psalm 4
To the chief Musician. On stringed instruments.
A psalm of David

1 When I call*, answer me, O God of my righteousness: in pressure you have enlarged me; be gracious to me, and hear my prayer.
2 You sons of men, till when is my glory [to be put] to shame? [How long] will you seek after a lie? Selah.
3 But know that Jehovah has set apart the pious *(chasid)* [man] for himself; Jehovah will hear when I call to him
4 Be moved with anger~ and don't sin; meditate in your own hearts upon your bed and be still. Selah.
5 Offer^ sacrifices of righteousness and confide+ in Jehovah.
6 Many say, "Who shall cause us to see good?" Lift up the light of your countenance upon us, o Jehovah.
7 You have put joy in my heart, more than in the time that their corn and their new wine was in abundance.
8 In peace I will both lay me down and sleep; for you, Jehovah, alone make me to dwell in safety.^^

* It is abstract 'in my calling'. Same in v3   ~ or 'tremble'   ^ as in Exodus 23v18
+ implying 'security without anxiety', same in other psalms
^^ Or 'for you, Jehovah make me [although] alone [yet] to dwell'

Psalm 5

To the chief Musician. Upon Nehiloth.
A psalm of David

1 Give ear to my words, o Jehovah; consider my meditation.
2 Hearken to the voice of my crying, my king and my God; for to you I will pray.
3 Jehovah, in the morning you shall hear my voice; in the morning I will address myself to you and will look up*.
4 For you are not a God that has pleasure in wickedness; evil~ shall not sojourn with you.
5 Insolent fools^ shall not stand before your eyes; you hate all workers of iniquity.
6 You will destroy those that speak lies: Jehovah abhors a man of blood and deceit.
7 But as for me, in the greatness of your loving-kindness I will enter your house; I will bow down with fear of you toward the temple of your holiness.
8 Lead me, Jehovah, in your righteousness, because of my foes; make your way plain before me.
9 For there is no certainty in their mouth; their inward part is perversion; their throat is an open sepulchre; they flatter with+ their tongue.
10 Bring guilt upon them, o God; let them fall by their own counsels: drive them out in the multitude of their transgressions for they have rebelled against you.
11 And all that trust in you shall rejoice; they shall shout joyously forever, and you will protect them; and they that love your name shall exult in you.
12 For you, Jehovah, will bless the righteous [man]; you will surround him with favour as [with] a shield.

* with the sense of waiting, expectancy   ~ or 'the evil man'
^ or 'the boastful or 'the arrogant'   + literally 'make smooth'

Psalm 6
To the chief Musician. On stringed instruments, upon Sheminith.
A psalm of David

1 Jehovah, don't rebuke me in your anger and don't chasten me in your hot displeasure.
2 Be gracious to me, Jehovah, for I am withered; Jehovah, heal me, for my bones tremble.
3 And my soul exceedingly trembles; and you, Jehovah, till how long?
4 Return, Jehovah, free my soul; save me for your loving-kindness' *(chesed)* sake.
5 For in death there is no remembrance of you; in Sheol who shall give thanks to you?*
6 I am wearied with my groaning; all the night I make my bed to swim; I dissolve my couch with my tears.
7 My eye wastes away through grief; it has grown old because of all my oppressors *(tzar)*.
8 Depart from me, all you workers of iniquity; for Jehovah has heard the voice of my weeping.
9 Jehovah has heard my supplication; Jehovah receives my prayer.
10 All my enemies shall be ashamed and exceedingly tremble; they will turn; they will be suddenly ashamed.

* or 'celebrate your praises'

Psalm 7

Shiggaion of David, which he sang to Jehovah,
concerning the words of Cush the Benjaminite

1 Jehovah my God, I have trusted in you: save me from all my pursuers, and deliver me;
2 in case he tears my soul like a lion, crushing it while there is no deliverer.
3 Jehovah my God, if I have done this, if there is iniquity in my hands;
4 if I have rewarded evil to him who was at peace with me (indeed, I have freed him that* oppressed me without cause);
5 let the enemy pursue after my soul and take [it], and let him tread down my life to the earth and lay my glory~ in the dust. Selah.
6 Arise, Jehovah, in your anger; lift yourself up against the raging of my oppressors and awake for me; you have commanded judgment.
7 And the assembly of the peoples shall encompass you; and for their sakes^ return on high.
8 Jehovah shall minister judgment to the peoples *(ammim)*. Judge me, Jehovah, according to my righteousness, and according to my integrity which is in me+.
9 Oh let the wrong of the wicked come to an end, and may you establish the righteous [man]; even you, the righteous God, who tries the hearts and reins.
10 My shield is with God, who saves the upright in heart.
11 God is a righteous judge^^ and a God who is indignant all the day**.
12 If one ++ turn not, he will sharpen his sword; he has bent his bow and made it ready~~,
13 and he has prepared for him 1 instruments of death; he has made his arrows to burn.
14 Behold, he travails with iniquity, yes, he has conceived mischief, and brought forth falsehood:
15 he has dug a pit and hollowed it out, and he has fallen into the hole that he made.
16 His mischief shall return upon his own head and his violence shall come down upon his own pate.
17 I will praise Jehovah according to his righteousness and will sing forth the name of Jehovah the Most High.

---

* or 'have despoiled him who'   ~ or 'cause my honour to dwell' ^ or 'above it'
+ or 'be it done to me'   ^^ or 'God judges the righteous'   ** or 'angry in every day'
++ or 'if he' i.e. 'the wicked one) ~~ or 'adjusted it' 1 or 'pointed at him'

Psalm 8
To the chief Musician. Upon the Gittith.
A psalm of David

1 Jehovah our Lord, how excellent is your name in all the earth! ...who has set* your majesty above the heavens.
2 Out of the mouth of babes and sucklings you have established praise ~ because of your adversaries *(tzar)*, to still the enemy^ and the avenger.
3 When I see your heavens, the work of your fingers, the moon and the stars, which you have established;
4 what is man *(Enosh)* that you are mindful of him? And the son of man *(Adam)*, that you visit+ him?
5 You have made him a little lower than the angels^^, and have crowned him with glory and splendour.
6 You have made him to rule over the works of your hands; you have put everything under his feet:
7 sheep and oxen, all of them, and also the beasts of the field;
8 the fowl of the heavens, and the fishes of the sea, [whatever] passes through the paths of the seas.
9 Jehovah our Lord, how excellent is your name in all the earth!

* possibly the imperative tense, so '...earth! because of which, set your   majesty...'
~ or 'founded strength'   ^ oyeb   + or 'regard'   ^^ *Elohim* (also in Ps97v7)

Psalm 9

To the chief Musician. Upon Muthlabben.
A psalm of David

1 I will praise you with my whole heart; I will recount all your marvellous works.
2 I will be glad and rejoice in you; I will sing forth your name, o Most High.
3 When my enemies turned back, they stumbled and perished at your presence:
4 for you have maintained my right and my cause. You sit on the throne, judging righteously.
5 You have rebuked the nations, you have destroyed the wicked*; you have put out their name for ever and ever.
6 O enemy! Destructions are ended for ever - you have also destroyed cities, even the remembrance of them has perished~.
7 But Jehovah sits for ever; he has ordained his throne for judgment.
8 And it is he that will judge the world *(tebel)* with righteousness; he shall execute judgment upon the peoples with equity.
9 And Jehovah will be a refuge^ to the oppressed one, a refuge^ in times of distress.
10 And they that know your name will confide in you; for you, Jehovah, have not forsaken them that seek you.
11 Sing psalms to Jehovah who dwells in Zion; tell among the people his doings.
12 For when he makes inquisition for blood, he+ remembers them; the cry of the afflicted ones he has not forgotten.
13 Be gracious to me, o Jehovah; consider my affliction from them that hate me, lifting^^ me up from the gates of death:
14 that I may declare all your praise in the gates of the daughter of Zion. I will be joyful in your salvation.
15 The nations are sunk down in the pit [that] they made; in the net that they hid their own foot is taken.
16 Jehovah is known [by] the judgment he has executed: the wicked is ensnared in the work of his own hands. Higgaion. Selah
17 The wicked shall be turned into Sheol, all the nations that forget God.

---

* the word is singular and therefore characteristic; same in v16; plural in v17
~ or 'their memorial has perished [along with them], or 'even theirs'
^ strictly 'a high fortress', 'high tower'   + or 'For he that requires blood'
^^ or 'you that lifts'

18 For the needy shall not always be forgotten; the hope of the meek** shall not perish for ever.
19 Arise, Jehovah; let not man *(Enosh)* prevail: let the nations be judged in your sight.
20 Put them in fear, Jehovah: that the nations may know themselves to be but men *(Enosh)*. Selah.

** or 'the afflicted ones' – it's plural. 'meek' and 'afflicted' are connected in Hebrew

Psalm 10

1 Why Jehovah, do you stand far off? [Why] do you hide yourself in times of distress?
2 The wicked, in his pride, hotly pursues the afflicted*. They shall be taken in the devices that they have imagined.
3 For the wicked boasts of his soul's desire and blesses the covetous; he contemns Jehovah.
4 The wicked [says], in the haughtiness of his countenance, 'He does not search out"~: all his thoughts are, "There is no God!"
5 His ways always succeed^; your judgments are far above out of his sight; [as for] all his adversaries, he puffs at them.
6 He says in his heart, "I shall not be moved; from generation to generation I shall be in no adversity".
7 His mouth is full of cursing and deceit and oppression; under his tongue is mischief and iniquity.
8 He sits in the lurking-places of the villages; he slays the innocent in the secret places: his eyes watch for the wretched.
9 He lies in wait secretly, like a lion in his thicket; he lies in wait to catch the afflicted: he catches the afflicted, drawing them into his net.
10 He crouches, he bows down, that the wretched may fall by his strong ones+.
11 He says in his heart, "God has forgotten, he hides his face, he will never see [it]".
12 Arise, Jehovah: o God, lift up your hand: don't forget the afflicted.^^
13 Wherefore does the wicked contemn God? He has said in his heart, "You will not require [it]".
14 You have seen [it], for you yourself behold trouble** and vexation, to requite by~~ your hand. The wretched commits himself++ to you; you have been the helper of the fatherless.
15 Break the arm of the wicked, and as for the evil man, seek out his wickedness [till] you find none.
16 Jehovah is king for ever and ever: the nations have perished out of his land.
17 Jehovah, you have heard the desire of the meek, you have established their heart: you cause your ear to hear,
18 to do justice to the fatherless and the oppressed one, that the man *(Enosh)* of the earth may terrify no more.

---

* or 'Through the pride of the wicked [man], the afflicted is sore pressed
~ or 'The wicked in his haughtiness does not seek [God], or 'troubles himself for nothing'   ^ or 'are rigid'   + An allusion probably to 'fangs' [of a lion]   ^^ others translate 'the meek'   ** or 'mischief'   ~~ or 'to put it into   ++ or 'commits it''

Psalm 11
To the chief Musician.
[A psalm] of David

1 In Jehovah have I put my trust: how say you to my soul, "Flee [as] a bird to your mountain"?
2 For behold, the wicked bend the bow, they make ready the arrow upon the string, that they may in darkness shoot at the upright in heart.
3 If the foundations are destroyed, what shall the righteous do?
4 Jehovah is in the temple of his holiness; Jehovah – his throne is in the heavens: his eyes behold, his eyelids try the children of men.
5 Jehovah tries the righteous one; but the wicked, and he that loves violence, his soul hates.
6 Upon the wicked he shall rain snares, fire and brimstone; and scorching wind shall be* the portion of their cup.
7 For Jehovah is righteous; he loves righteousness~, his countenance beholds the upright^.

* or 'snares: fire and brimstone and a scorching wind shall be...'
~ literally 'righteousnesses'   ^ or 'the upright shall see his face'

Psalm 12
To the chief Musician. Upon Sheminith.
A psalm of David

1 Save, Jehovah, for the godly man is gone*; for the faithful have failed from among the children of men.
2 Each one speaks falsehood~ with his neighbour: they speak [with] a flattering lip, with a double heart.
3 Jehovah will cut off all flattering lips, the tongue that speaks proud^ things,
4 who have said, "We will prevail with our tongue, our lips are our own: who [is] lord over us?"
5 Because of the oppression of the afflicted, because of the sighing of the needy, I will now arise, says Jehovah; the one at whom they puff+ I will set in safety.
6 The words *(imrah)* of Jehovah are pure words *(imrah)*, silver tried in the furnace of earth, purified seven times.
7 You, Jehovah, will keep them, you will preserve them^^ from this generation for ever.
8 The wicked walk about on every side when vileness is exalted among the children of men.

* or 'ceases'   ~ or 'vanity'   ^ or 'great' + Lit "at whom one puffs"   ^^ or 'him'

Psalm 13
To the chief Musician
A psalm of David

1 How long, Jehovah, will you forget me for ever? How long will you hide your face from me?
2 How long shall I take counsel in my soul, with sorrow in my heart daily? How long shall my enemy be exalted over me?
3 Consider, answer me, O Jehovah my God! Lighten my eyes in case I sleep the [sleep of] death;
4 in case my enemy say, "I have prevailed against him!", [in case] my adversaries be joyful when I am moved.
5 As for me, I have confided in your loving-kindness(*chesed*); my heart shall be joyful in your salvation.
6 I will sing to Jehovah, for he has dealt bountifully with me.

Psalm 14*
To the chief Musician.
[A psalm] of David

1 The fool~ has said in his heart, "There is no God". They have corrupted themselves, they have done abominable works: there is none that does good.
2 Jehovah looked down from the heavens upon the children of men, to see if there were any that did understand, that did seek God.
3 They have all gone aside, they are together^ become corrupt; there is none that does good, not even one.
4 Have all the workers of iniquity no knowledge, eating up my people [as] they that eat bread? They don't call upon Jehovah.
5 There they were in great fear; for God is in the generation of the righteous.
6 You have shamed the counsel of the afflicted because Jehovah [was] his refuge.
7 Oh that the salvation of Israel would come out of Zion! When Jehovah turns again the captivity+ of his people, Jacob shall be glad, Israel shall rejoice.

* compare psalm 53   ~ nabal
^ that is, as a collective group, or possibly "have together"
+ strictly, "the turning" or "the returning" in the sense of complete restoration and establishment of full blessing; in psalm 126 v1

Psalm 15
A psalm of David

1 Jehovah, who shall sojourn in your tent? Who shall dwell in the hill of your holiness?
2 He that walks uprightly, and works righteousness, and speaks the truth from his heart.
3 He that does not slander with his tongue and does not do evil to his companion, nor takes up a reproach against his neighbour;
4 in whose eyes the depraved person is contemned and who honours them that fear Jehovah; who, if he has sworn to his own hurt, does not change;
5 [he that] does not put out his money to usury, nor takes reward* against the innocent. He that does these [things] shall never be moved.

* or 'a bribe'

Psalm 16
Michtam of David

1 Preserve me, o God: for I trust in you.
2 [my soul] you have said to Jehovah, "You are the Lord: my goodness does not [extend] to you":
3 to the saints* that are on the earth, and to the excellent [you have said], "In them is all my delight".
4 Their sorrows shall be multiplied that hasten after another: I will not offer their drink-offerings of blood, and I will not take up their names into my lips.
5 Jehovah is the portion of my inheritance~ and of my cup: you maintain my lot.
6 The lines^ have fallen+ to me in pleasant places; yes, I have a goodly heritage.
7 I will bless Jehovah, who gives me counsel: even in the nights my reins instruct me.
8 I have set Jehovah before me: because [he is] at my right hand, I shall not be moved.
9 Therefore my heart rejoices and my glory^^ exults: my flesh moreover shall dwell in hope**.
10 For you will not leave my soul to Sheol, neither will you allow your Holy One~~ to see corruption.
11 You will make known to me the path of life: your countenance is fulness of joy; at your right hand are pleasures for evermore.

---

* *kadoshim* (plural of *kadosh*); when used of God in other psalms, translated 'holy', 'holy one'
~ or 'my assigned portion'   ^ or 'portions'
+ see Micah 2v5 which refers to "cast the measuring line upon a lot"
^^ or 'honour'; can be used as a synonym of 'soul'; in Acts 2v26 'tongue'
** or 'shall rest in safety'   ~~ or 'gracious one' *chasid*

Psalm 17
A prayer of David

1 Hear the right*, O Jehovah, attend to my cry; give ear to my prayer which is not out of feigned lips.
2 Let my judgment~ come forth from your presence, let your eyes regard equity.
3 You have proved my heart, you have visited me by night; you have tried me, you have found nothing: my thought does not go beyond my word.
4 Concerning the works of men, by the word of your lips I have kept from^ the paths of the violent [man].
5 When you hold my goings in your paths, my footsteps don't slip.
6 I have called upon you, for you answer me, o God. Incline your ear to me, hear my speech *(imrah)*.
7 Wondrously show your loving-kindnesses *(chesed)*, o you who saves by your right hand them that trust [in you] from those that rise up [against them].
8 Keep me as the apple of the eye+, hide me under the shadow of your wings,
9 from the wicked that destroy me, my deadly enemies, who compass me about.
10 They are enclosed in their own fat; with their mouth they speak proudly.
11 They have now encompassed us in our steps; they have set their eyes, bowing down to the earth^^.
12 He is like a lion that is greedy of its prey, and as a young lion lurking in secret places.
13 Arise, Jehovah, anticipate him, cast him down: deliver my soul from the wicked, your sword**;
14 from men [who are]~~ your hand, o Jehovah, from men of this age++: their portion is in [this] life, and you fill their belly with your hidden [treasure]; they have their fill of sons 1, and leave the rest of their substance to their children.
15 As for me, I will behold your face in righteousness; I shall be satisfied, when I awake, with 2 your likeness.

---

* strictly 'righteousness'   ~ or 'right'   ^ or 'I have paid attention to'
+ Deuteronomy 32 v10, Proverbs 7 v2,9; Proverbs 20 v20
^^ or 'they set their eyes to cast [us] down to the earth'
** or '[by] their sword'   ~~ or '[by]' instead of [who are]
++ *cheled* – 'world' (Ps49) or 'life' (Ps89 v47) or 'lifetime' (Ps39 v5)
1 or '[their] sons are surfeited'   2 or 'as'

Psalm 18

To the chief Musician.
[A psalm] of David, the servant of Jehovah,
who spoke to Jehovah the words of this song in the day that
Jehovah had delivered him out of the hand of all his enemies*
and out of the hand of Saul~

1 I will love you, o Jehovah, my strength.

2 Jehovah is my rock 1, and my fortress, and my deliverer; my God, my rock, in whom I will trust; my shield, and the horn of my salvation, my high tower.

3 I will call upon Jehovah, who is to be praised: so shall I be saved from my enemies.

4 The bands of death encompassed me, and torrents of Belial made me afraid.

5 The bands of Sheol surrounded me, the cords of death encountered me.

6 In my distress I called upon jehovah, and I cried out to my God; he heard my voice out of his temple, and my cry came before him into his ears.

7 Then the earth shook and quaked, the foundations of the mountains trembled and shook because he was wroth.

8 There went up a smoke out of his nostrils, and fire out of his mouth devoured: coals burned forth from it.

9 And he bowed the heavens, and came down, and darkness was under his feet.

10 And he rode upon a cherub and did fly; yes, he flew fast upon the wings of the wind.

11 He made darkness his secret place, his tent round about him: darkness of waters, thick clouds of the skies.

12 From the brightness before him his thick clouds passed forth: hail and coals of fire.

13 And Jehovah thundered in the heavens, and the Most High uttered his voice: hail and coals of fire.

14 And he sent his arrows, and scattered [my enemies] 2 ; and he shot forth lightnings 3 ; and discomfited them.

15 And the beds of the waters were seen, and the foundations of the world were uncovered at your rebuke, Jehovah, at the blast of your nostrils.

16 He reached forth from above, he took me, he drew me out of great waters:

---

* *oyeb* – external enemy   ~ See 2 Samuel 22 for context, and where most of this psalm can be found   1 sela – 'a high rock'; and again in verses 3,17,37,40,48; also in Psalm 31 v3   2 literally 'and scattered them'   3 or 'and many lightnings'

17 he delivered me from my strong enemy, and from them that hated me: for they were mightier than I.
18 They encountered me in the day of my calamity, but Jehovah was my stay.
19 And he brought me forth into a large place; he delivered me because he delighted in me.
20 Jehovah has rewarded me according to my righteousness; according to the cleanness of my hands he has recompensed me.
21 For I have kept the ways of Jehovah, and have not wickedly departed from my God.
22 For all his ordinances 4 were before me, and I did not put away his statutes from me;
23 and I was 5 upright with him, and kept myself from my iniquity.
24 And Jehovah has recompensed me according to my righteousness, according to the cleanness of my hands in his sight.
25 With the gracious 6, you show yourself gracious 7 ; with the upright man you show yourself upright;
26 with the pure you show yourself pure; and with the perverse you show yourself contrary.
27 For it is you that 8 saves the afflicted people; but you will bring down the haughty eyes.
28 For it is you that makes my lamp to shine: Jehovah my God enlightens my darkness.
29 For by you I have run through a troop: and by my God I have leaped over a wall.
30 As for God, his way is perfect; the word *(imrah)* of Jehovah is tried 9: he is a shield to all that trust in him.
31 For who is God except Jehovah? And who is a rock if not our God?
32 The God who girds me with strength, and makes my way perfect,
33 who makes my feet like hinds' [feet], and sets me upon my high places:
34 who teaches my hand to war, and my arms bend a bow of brass;
35 and you gave me the shield of your salvation, and your right hand held me up; and your condescending greatness has made me great.
36 You enlarged my steps under me, and my ankles have not wavered.

---

4 or 'judgments'   5 or 'perfect'   6 *chasid*   7 *chesed*
8 or 'will save'   9 or 'refined' (see Psalm 12 v6)

37 I pursued my enemies and overtook them; and I didn't turn again till they were consumed.
38 I crushed them, and they were not able to rise: they fell under my feet.
39 And you girded me with strength to battle; you subdued under me those that rose up against me.
40 And you made my enemies to turn their back to me, and those that hated me I destroyed.
41 They cried and their was none to save; to Jehovah, and he didn't answer them.
42 And I beat them small as dust before the wind: I cast them out as the mire of the streets.
43 You have delivered me from the strivings of the people; you have made me to be the head of the nations: a people I did not know serves me.
44 At the hearing of the ear, they obey me: strangers come cringing to me.
45 Strangers have faded away, and they come trembling forth from their close 10 places.
46 Jehovah lives; and blessed be my rock; and exalted be the God of my salvation,
47 the God who has avenged me, and has subjected the peoples to me;
48 who has delivered me from my enemies: yes, you have lifted me up above them that rose up against me; from the man of violence you have delivered me.
49 Therefore I will give thanks to you, Jehovah, among the nations, and will sing psalms to your name.
50 [It is he] who gives great deliverances to his king, and shows loving-kindness *(chesed)* to his anointed, to David, and to his seed for evermore.

---

10 or 'fortified'

Psalm 19

To the chief Musician.
A psalm of David

1 The heavens declare the glory of God; and the expanse shows the work of his hands.
2 Day unto day utters speech* and night unto night shows knowledge.
3 There is no speech and there are no words, yet their voice is heard.
4 Their line~ is gone out through all the earth and their language to the extremity of the world. In them has he set a tent for the sun,
5 and he is as a bridegroom going forth from his chamber; he rejoices as a strong man to run the race.
6 His going forth^ is from the end of the heavens, and his circuit to the ends of it; and there is nothing hid from its heat.
7 The law of Jehovah is perfect, restoring the soul; the testimony of Jehovah is sure, making the simple wise;
8 the precepts of Jehovah are right, rejoicing the heart; the commandment of Jehovah is pure, enlightening the eyes;
9 the fear of Jehovah is clean, enduring for ever; the judgments of Jehovah are truth, they are righteous altogether:
10 they are more precious than gold, yes, than much fine gold; and sweeter than honey and the dropping of the honeycomb.
11 Moreover, by them your servant is enlightened; in keeping them there is great reward.
12 Who understands [his] errors? Purify+ me from secret [faults].
13 Keep back your servant also from presumptuous [sins^^]; don't let them have dominion over me: then I shall be perfect and I shall be innocent from great transgression**.
14 Let the words of my mouth and the meditation of my heart be acceptable in your sight, o Jehovah, my rock, and my redeemer.

---

* literally, 'causes to boil forth', 'gush' (as of a stream); also in Psalm 145 v7
~ meaning the 'extent' of their testimony   ^ or 'starting'   + or 'clear'
^^ or 'from the presumptuous'   ** or 'from the great transgression'

Psalm 20
To the chief Musician.
A psalm of David

1 Jehovah answer you in the day of trouble; the name of the God of Jacob protect you*;
2 may he send you help from the sanctuary and strengthen you out of Zion;
3 remember all your oblations and accept~ your burnt offering; Selah.
4 grant you according to your heart and fulfil all your counsels.
5 We will triumph in your salvation and in the name of our God we will set up our banners. May Jehovah fulfil all your petitions!
6 Now I know that Jehovah saves his anointed; he answers him from the heavens of his holiness, with the saving strength of his right hand.
7 Some make mention of chariots and some of horses, but we of the name of Jehovah our God.
8 They are bowed down and fallen; but we are risen and stand upright.
9 Save, Jehovah! Let the king answer us when we call^.

* or 'set you up on high'
~ or 'turn to ashes', or 'let your burnt offering be fat to him'
^ or 'Let Jehovah save the king. Let him answer...etc'

Psalm 21
To the chief Musician.
A psalm of David

1 The king shall joy in your strength, Jehovah; and in your salvation how greatly shall he rejoice.
2 You have given him his heart's desire and have not withheld the request of his lips. Selah.
3 For you have met him with the blessings of goodness; you have set a crown of pure gold on his head.
4 He asked life of you; you gave [it] him, length of days for ever and ever.
5 His glory is great through your salvation; majesty and splendour have you laid upon him.
6 For you have made him to be blessings for ever; you have filled him with joy by your countenance.
7 For the king confides in Jehovah: and through the loving-kindness of the Most High he shall not be moved.
8 Your right hand shall find out all your enemies; your right hand shall find out those that hate you.
9 You shall make them as a fiery furnace in the time of your presence; Jehovah shall swallow them up in his anger, and the fire shall devour them:
10 their fruit you shall destroy from the earth, and their seed from among the children of men.
11 For they intended* evil against you; they imagined a mischievous device which they could not execute.
12 For you will make them turn their back; you will make ready your bowstring against their face.
13 Be exalted, Jehovah, in your own strength: we will sing and celebrate your power.

* Literally 'spread out', as in 'extend'

Psalm 22

To the chief Musician. Upon Aijeleth-Shahar.
A psalm of David

1 My God, my God, why have you forsaken me? [Why are you] far from my salvation?
2 My God, I cry by day, and you don't answer; and by night, and there is no rest for me:
3 and you are holy, you that dwells amid the praises of Israel.
4 Our fathers confided in you, and you delivered them.
5 They cried to you and were delivered; they confided in you and were not confounded.
6 But I am a worm and no man; a reproach of men and the despised of the people.
7 All they that see me laugh me to scorn; they shoot out the lip, they shake the head, [saying:]
8 "Commit it to* Jehovah – let him rescue him; let him deliver him, because he delights in him!"
9 But you are he that took me out of the womb; you did make me trust, upon my mother's breasts.
10 I was cast upon you from the womb; you are my God from my mother's belly.
11 Don't be far from me, for trouble is near; for there is none to help.
12 Many~ bulls have encompassed me; Bashan's strong ones surround me.
13 They gape upon me with their mouth, [as] a ravening and roaring lion.
14 I am poured out like water and all my bones are out of joint: my heart has become like wax; it is melted in the centre of my bowels.
15 My strength is dried up like a potsherd and my tongue cleaves to my palate; and you have laid me in the dust of death.
16 For dogs have encompassed me; an assembly of evildoers have surrounded me: they pierced my hands and my feet.
17 I may count^ all my bones. They look, they stare upon me;
18 they part my garments among them and cast lots upon my vesture.
19 But you, Jehovah, don't be far [from me]; o my strength, hasten to help me.
20 Deliver my soul from the sword; my only one from the power+ of the dog;

---

* literally 'roll it on' or 'roll himself on'   ~ or 'great'   ^ or 'I count'
+ Literally 'the hand'

21 save me from the lion's mouth. Yes, from the horns of the buffaloes you have answered me.
22 I will declare your name to my brethren, in the midst of the congregation I will praise you.
23 You that fear Jehovah, praise him; all you the seed of Jacob, glorify him; and revere him, all you the seed of Israel.
24 For he has not despised nor abhorred the affliction of the afflicted; neither has he hid his face from him: but when he cried to him, he heard.
25 My praise is from you, in the great congregation; I will pay my vows before them that fear him.
26 The meek shall eat and be satisfied; they shall praise Jehovah that seek him: your heart shall live for ever.
27 All the ends of the earth shall remember and turn to Jehovah and all the families of the nations shall worship before you:
28 for the kingdom is Jehovah's and he rules among the nations.
29 All the fat ones of the earth shall eat and worship; all they that go down to the dust shall bow before him and he that cannot keep alive his own soul.
30 A seed shall serve him; it shall be accounted to the Lord for a generation^^.
31 They shall come and shall declare his righteousness to a people that shall be born, that he has done [it].

^^ or 'it shall be told concerning the Lord to the [coming] generation

Psalm 23
A psalm of David

1 Jehovah is my shepherd; I shall not want.
2 He makes me to lie down in green pastures; he leads me beside still waters.
3 He restores* my soul; he leads me in paths of righteousness for his name's sake.
4 Yes, though I walk through the valley of the shadow of death, I will fear no evil: for you are with me; your rod and your staff they comfort me.
5 You prepare~ a table before me in the presence of my enemies; you have anointed my head with oil; my cup runs over.
6 Surely^, goodness and loving-kindness shall follow me all the days of my life; and I will dwell in the house of Jehovah for the length of the days

* or 'revives'   ~ or 'furnish'   ^ or 'only'

Psalm 24
Of David. A psalm

1 The earth is Jehovah's and its fulness; the world *(tebel)* and they that dwell in it.
2 For it was he that founded it upon seas and established it upon floods.
3 Who shall ascend into the mount of Jehovah? And who shall stand in his holy place?
4 He that has blameless* hands and a pure heart; who does not lift up his soul to vanity, nor swear deceitfully:
5 he shall receive blessing from Jehovah and righteousness from the God of his salvation.
6 This is the generation of them that seek him, that seek your face, O Jacob~. Selah.
7 Lift up your heads, you gates, and be lifted up, you everlasting doors, and the king of glory shall come in.
8 Who is this king of glory? Jehovah strong and mighty, Jehovah mighty in battle.
9 Lift up your heads, you gates; yes, lift up, you everlasting doors, and the king of glory shall come in.
10 Who is he, this king of glory? Jehovah of hosts, he is the king of glory. Selah.

* or 'innocent'   ~ or 'your face [in] Jacob

Psalm 25*
[A psalm] of David

1 To you, Jehovah, do I lift up my soul.
2 My God, I confide in you; don't let me be ashamed or let my enemies triumph over me.
3 Yes, none that waits on you shall be ashamed; they shall be ashamed that deal treacherously without cause.
4 Make me to walk in your paths, o Jehovah; teach me your paths.
5 Make me to walk in your truth and teach me: for you are the God of my salvation; on you I wait all the day~.
6 Remember, Jehovah, your tender mercies and your loving-kindnesses; for they are from everlasting.
7 Don't remember the sins of my youth, nor my transgressions; according to your loving-kindness remember me, for your goodness sake, Jehovah.
8 Good and upright is Jehovah; therefore he will instruct sinners in the way:
9 the meek he will guide in judgment, and he will teach the meek his way.
10 All the paths of Jehovah are loving-kindness and truth for such as keep his covenant and his testimonies.
11 For your name's sake, o Jehovah, you will indeed pardon my iniquity; for it is great.
12 What man is he that fears Jehovah? He will instruct him in the way [that] he should choose^.
13 His soul shall dwell in prosperity and his seed shall inherit the earth+.
14 The secret of Jehovah is with them that fear him, that he may make known his covenant to them^^.
15 My eyes are ever toward Jehovah; for he will bring my feet out of the net.
16 Turn toward me and be gracious to me; for I am solitary and afflicted.
17 The troubles of my heart are increased: bring** me out of my distresses;
18 consider my affliction and my travail, and forgive all my sins.

---

* acrostic psalm: in alphabetical order, each verse begins with the relevant Hebrew letter   ~ or 'every day'   ^ or 'that He [Jehovah] chooses
+ or 'possess the land' – same as in Psalm 37 v9,29
^^ or 'and his covenant – to make them know [it]'
** other versions read, 'Relieve the troubles of my heart and bring...'

19 Consider my enemies, for they are many, and they hate me [with] cruel hatred.
20 Keep my soul and deliver me: don't let me be ashamed; for I trust in you.
21 Let integrity and uprightness~~ preserve me; for I wait on you.
22 Redeem Israel, o God, out of all his troubles.

~~ or 'Integrity (perfection) and uprightness shall'

Psalm 26
[A psalm] of David

1 Judge me, o Jehovah, for I have walked in my integrity, and I have confided in Jehovah: I shall not slip*.
2 Prove me, Jehovah, and test me; try my reins and my heart:
3 for your loving-kindness is before my eyes, and I have walked in your truth.
4 I have not sat with vain~ persons, neither have I gone in with dissemblers;
5 I have hated the congregation of evildoers and I have not sat^ with the wicked.
6 I will wash my hands in innocency and will encompass your altar, o Jehovah,
7 that I may cause the voice of thanksgiving to be heard and declare all your marvellous works.
8 Jehovah, I have loved the habitation of your house and the place where your glory dwells.
9 Don't gather my soul with sinners, nor my life with men of blood;
10 in whose hands are evil devices and their right hand is full of bribes.
11 But as for me, I will walk in my integrity. Redeem me and be gracious to me.
12 My foot stands in an even place; in the congregation I will bless Jehovah.

* or 'totter', 'waver'   ~ or 'false'   ^ or 'I will not sit...'

Psalm 27
[A psalm]of David

1 Jehovah is my light and my salvation; whom shall I fear?
Jehovah is the strength of my life; of whom shall I be afraid?*
2 When evildoers, my adversaries and my enemies *(oyeb)*, came upon me to eat up my flesh, they stumbled and fell.
3 If a host encamps against me, my heart shall not fear; if war rise against me, in this I will be confident.
4 One [thing] I have asked of Jehovah, that I will seek after: that I may dwell in the house of Jehovah all the days of my life, to behold the beauty~ of Jehovah, and to inquire [of him] in his temple.
5 For in the day of evil he will hide me in his pavilion; in the secret of his tent he will keep me concealed: he will set me high upon a rock.
6 And now my head shall be lifted up above my enemies round about me; and I will offer in his tent sacrifices of shouts of joy: I will sing, yes, I will sing psalms to Jehovah.
7 Hear, Jehovah; with my voice I call; be gracious to me and answer me.
8 My heart said for you, "Seek my face." Your face, o Jehovah, I will seek.
9 Don't hide your face from me; don't put your servant away in anger: you have been my help; don't cast me off, nor forsake me, o God of my salvation.
10 For had my mother and father forsaken me, then Jehovah would have taken me up^.
11 Teach me your way, Jehovah, and lead me in an even path, because of my enemies+.
12 Don't deliver me over to the will of my adversaries; for false witnesses have risen up against me, and such as breathe out violence.
13 Unless I had believed to see the goodness of Jehovah in the land of the living...!
14 Wait for Jehovah; be strong and let your heart take courage:^^ yes, wait for Jehovah.

---

* 'fear' and 'be afraid' are nearly the same, but 'be afraid' seems more like 'terror' and is used of Jehovah (e.g. Psalm 36 v1); 'fear' is usually more in a godly sense; in verse 3 it means simple 'fear'
~ or 'pleasantness'
^ or 'For my father and my mother have forsaken me, but Jehovah has gathered me'
+ or 'those that lie in wait for me'   ^^ or 'he will strengthen your heart'

Psalm 28
[A psalm] of David

1 To you, Jehovah, I call; my rock, don't be silent to me, in case [if] you keep silence toward me, I become like them that go down into the pit.
2 Hear the voice of my supplications, when I cry to you, when I lift up my hands toward the oracle of your holiness.
3 Don't draw me away with the wicked and with the workers of iniquity, who speak peace to their neighbours and mischief is in their heart.
4 Give them according to their doing, and according to the wickedness of their deeds; give them after the work of their hands, render to them what they deserve.
5 For* they don't regard the works of Jehovah nor the work of his hands: he will destroy them and not build them up.
6 Blessed be Jehovah, for he has heard the voice of my supplications.
7 Jehovah is my strength and my shield; my heart confided in him and I was helped: therefore my heart exults, and with my song I will praise him.
8 Jehovah is their strength; and he is the stronghold of salvation~ to his anointed one.
9 Save your people and bless your inheritance; and feed them, and lift^ them up for ever.

* or 'Because they don't regard the works of Jehovah....hands, he will destroy them...'
~ Literally 'salvations', 'deliverances' (compare Psalms 18 v50; 42 v5,11; 74 v12)
^ or 'bear'

Psalm 29
A psalm of David

1 Give* to Jehovah, you sons of the mighty ones, give* to Jehovah glory and strength.
2 Give* to Jehovah the glory of his name; worship Jehovah in holy splendour.
3 The voice of Jehovah is upon the waters: the God of glory thunders, – Jehovah upon great waters.
4 The voice of Jehovah is powerful; the voice of Jehovah is full of majesty.
5 The voice of Jehovah breaks cedars; yes, Jehovah breaks the cedars of Lebanon:
6 and he makes them to skip like a calf, Lebanon and Sirion~ like a young buffalo.
7 The voice of Jehovah cleaves out flames of fire.
8 The voice of Jehovah shakes the wilderness; Jehovah shakes the wilderness of Kadesh.
9 The voice of Jehovah makes the hinds to calve and lays bare the forests; and in his temple every one says^, "Glory!"
10 Jehovah sits upon the flood +; yes, Jehovah sits as king for ever.
11 Jehovah will give strength to his people; Jehovah will bless his people with peace.

* same as 'ascribe' (as in Deuteronomy 32 v3)
~ or Hermon (in Deuteronomy 3 v9)   ^ or perhaps 'everything says'
+ In Genesis 6 v17 the word is used of the 'deluge'

Psalm 30
A psalm of David: dedication-song of the house

1 I will extol you, Jehovah: for you have delivered me* and have not made my enemies to rejoice over me.
2 Jehovah my God, I cried to you and you have healed me.
3 Jehovah, you have brought up my soul from Sheol, you have quickened me from among those that go down to the pit.
4 Sing psalms to Jehovah, you saints *(chasid)* of his, and give thanks in remembrance of his holiness~.
5 For a moment [is passed in] his anger, a life in his favour; at evening weeping comes for the night, and at morning there is rejoicing.
6 As for me, I said in my prosperity, "I shall never be moved".
7 Jehovah, by your favour, you have made my mountain to stand strong: you hid your face; I was troubled.
8 I called to you, Jehovah, and I made supplication to the Lord^:
9 "What profit is there in my blood, in my going down to the pit? Shall the dust praise+ you? Shall it declare your truth?"
10 Hear, o Jehovah, and be gracious to me; Jehovah, be my helper.
11 You have turned for me my mourning into dancing; you have loosed my sackcloth and girded me with gladness;
12 that my glory may sing psalms of you and not be silent. Jehovah my God, I will praise you for ever.

* strictly 'drawn me up' (as out of a well)
~ or 'celebrate his holy memorial' (i.e. his holy name)
^ many read 'Jehovah'   + or 'give thanks to'

Psalm 31

To the chief Musician.
A psalm of David

1 In you, Jehovah, I trust; let me never be ashamed: deliver me in your righteousness.
2 Incline your ear to me, deliver me speedily; be a strong rock to me, a house of defence to save me.
3 For you are my rock* and my fortress; and for your name's sake you will lead me and guide me.
4 Draw~ me out of the net that they have hidden for me; for you are my strength.
5 Into your hands I commit my spirit: you have redeemed me, Jehovah, God of truth.
6 I have hated them that observe vanities^; and as for me, I have confided in Jehovah.
7 I will be glad and rejoice in your loving-kindness, for you have seen my affliction; you have known the troubles of my soul,
8 and have not shut me up into the hand of the enemy: you have set my feet in a large place.
9 Be gracious to me, Jehovah, for I am in trouble: my eye wastes away with vexation, my soul and my belly.
10 For my life is spent with sighing; my strength fails through my iniquity+ and my bones are wasted.
11 More than to all^^ my oppressors, I have become exceedingly a reproach, even to my neighbours and a fear to my acquaintance: they that see me around** flee from me.
12 I am forgotten in~~ [their] heart as a dead man; I have become like a broken vessel.
13 For I have heard the slander of many – terror on every side – when they take counsel together against me: they plot to take away my life.
14 But I confided in you, Jehovah; I said, You are my God.
15 My times are in your hand: deliver me from the hand of my enemies and from my persecutors.
16 Make your face to shine upon your servant; save me in your loving-kindness.
17 Jehovah, don't let me be ashamed, for I have called upon you; let the wicked be ashamed, let them be silent in Sheol.

*high rock as in Psalm 18 v2   ~ or 'You will draw...'   ^ or 'vain idols'
+ or 'my misery (distress)' but meaning 'punishment'
^^ or 'Because of all...'
** Darby uses 'without'; my preference 'around' rather than 'outside' because it's more encompassing   ~~ literally 'from'

18 Let the lying lips become dumb, which speak insolently against the righteous in pride and contempt.
19 [Oh] how great is your goodnes, which you have laid up for them that fear you, [which] you have wrought for them that trust in you, before the sons of men!
20 You keep them concealed in the secret of your presence from the conspiracies of man; you hide++ them in a pavilion from the strife of tongues.
21 Blessed be Jehovah for he has shown me wondrously his loving-kindness in a strong city.
22 As for me, I said in my haste 1, I am cut off from before your eyes; nevertheless, you heard the voice of my supplications when I cried to you.
23 Love Jehovah, all you his saints *[chasid]*. Jehovah preserves the faithful and plentifully requites the proud doer.
24 Be strong, and let your heart take courage, all you that hope in Jehovah.

++ 'hidden ones' is referenced in Psalm 83 v3
1 or 'agitation' or 'terror' or 'alarm'

Psalm 32
Of David. Instruction

1 Blessed is he [whose] transgression is forgiven, [whose] sin is covered!
2 Blessed is the man to whom Jehovah does not reckon iniquity, and in whose spirit there is no guile!
3 When I kept silence, my bones waxed old through my groaning all the day long.
4 For day and night your hand was heavy upon me; my moisture was turned into the drought of summer. Selah.
5 I acknowledged my sin to you, and I didn't cover my iniquity; I said, "I will confess my transgressions to Jehovah", and you forgave the iniquity of my sin. Selah.
6 For this shall every one that is godly *(chasid)* pray to you at a time when you may be found: surely in the floods of great waters they will not reach him.
7 You are a hiding place for me; you preserve me from trouble; you encompass me with songs of deliverance. Selah.
8 I will instruct you and teach you the way in which you shall go; I will counsel [you] with my eye upon you*.
9 Don't be as a horse, as a mule, which have no understanding: whose trappings must be a bit and bridle for restraint or they will not come near you~.
10 The wicked have many sorrows, but he that confides in Jehovah, loving-kindness shall encompass him.
11 Rejoice in Jehovah, you righteous; and shout for joy, all you upright in heart.

* or 'I will give counsel with...'   ~ or 'in case they come near...'

Psalm 33

1 Exult in Jehovah, you righteous: praise is comely for the upright.
2 Give thanks to Jehovah with the harp; sing psalms to him with the ten-stringed* lute.
3 Sing to him a new song; play skilfully with a loud sound.
4 For the word of Jehovah is right, and all his work is in faithfulness.
5 He loves righteousness and judgment~: the earth is full of the loving-kindness of Jehovah.
6 By the word of Jehovah the heavens were made, and all the host of them by the breath of his mouth.
7 He gathers the waters of the sea together as a heap; he lays up the deeps in storehouses.
8 Let all the earth fear Jehovah; let all the inhabitants of the world stand in awe^ of him.
9 For he spoke and it was [done]; he commanded and it stood fast.
10 Jehovah frustrates the counsel of the nations; he makes the thoughts of the peoples of none effect.
11 The counsel of Jehovah stands for ever, the thoughts of his heart from generation to generation.
12 Blessed is the nation whose God is Jehovah, the people that he has chosen for his inheritance!
13 Jehovah looks from the heavens; he beholds all the sons of men;
14 from the place+ of his habitation he looks forth upon all the inhabitants of the earth;
15 he who fashions the hearts of them all, who considers all their works.
16 The king is not saved by the multitude of [his] forces; a mighty man is not delivered by much strength.
17 The horse is a vain thing for safety; neither does it deliver by his great power.
18 Behold, the eye of Jehovah is upon them that fear him, upon them that hope in his loving-kindness,
19 to deliver their soul from death and to keep them alive in famine.
20 Our soul waits for Jehovah: he is our help and our shield.
21 For in him our heart shall rejoice because we have confided in his holy name.
22 Let your loving-kindness, o Jehovah, be upon us according as we have hoped in you.

* see Psalm 92 v3   ~ or 'justice'   ^ or 'revere'   +strictly 'settled place'

Psalm 34*

[A psalm] of David...when he changed his behaviour before Abimelech~, who drove him away, and he departed

1 I will bless Jehovah at all times; his praise shall continually be in my mouth.
2 My soul shall make its boast in Jehovah: the meek shall hear and rejoice.
3 Magnify Jehovah with me and let us exalt his name together.
4 I sought Jehovah and he answered me, and delivered me from all my fears.
5 They looked to him and were enlightened, and their faces were not^ confounded.
6 This afflicted one called and Jehovah heard [him] and saved him out of all his troubles.
7 The angel of Jehovah encamps round about them that fear him, and delivers them.
8 Taste and see that Jehovah is good: blessed is the man *(geber)* that trusts in him!
9 Fear Jehovah, you his saints; for there is no want to them that fear him.
10 The young lions are in need and suffer hunger; but they that seek Jehovah shall not want any good.
11 Come, sons, hearken to me: I will teach you the fear of Jehovah.
12 What man is he that desires life [and] loves days that he may see good?
13 keep your tongue from evil and your lips from speaking guile;
14 depart from evil and do good; seek peace and pursue it.
15 The eyes of Jehovah are upon the righteous, and his ears are toward their cry;
16 The face of Jehovah is against those that do evil, to cut off the remembrance of them from the earth:
17 [the righteous] cry and Jehovah hears and delivers them out of all their troubles.
18 Jehovah is near to those that are of a broken heart, and saves them that are of a contrite spirit.
19 Many are the adversities of the righteous but Jehovah delivers him out of them all:
20 he keeps all his bones; not one of them is broken.

* acrostic psalm   ~ means 'Father-king', most probably the usual title of the Philistine kings   ^ or 'shall not be'

21 Evil shall destroy+ the wicked; and they that hate the righteous shall bear their guilt^^.
22 Jehovah redeems the soul of his servants; and none of them that trust in him shall bear guilt^^.

+ or 'destroy utterly' (it's the intensive form of the verb)
^^ or 'shall be condemned'

Psalm 35
[A psalm] of David

1 Strive, o Jehovah, with those that strive with me; fight against them that fight against me:
2 take hold of shield and buckler and stand up for my help;
3 and draw out the spear, and stop [the way] against my pursuers: say to my soul, "I am your salvation".
4 Let them be put to shame and confounded that seek after my life*; let them be turned backward and brought to confusion that devise my hurt:
5 let them be as chaff before the wind, and let the angel of Jehovah drive [them] away;
6 let their way be dark and slippery, and let the angel of Jehovah pursue them.
7 For without cause they have hidden for me their net [in] a pit; without cause they have dug [it] for my soul.
8 Let destruction come upon him unawares, and let his net which he has hidden catch himself: for destruction let him fall into it.
9 And my soul shall be joyful in Jehovah: it shall rejoice in his salvation.
10 All my bones shall say, "Jehovah, who is like you, who delivers the afflicted from one stronger than himself, yes, the afflicted and the needy from him that spoils him!"
11 Unrighteous witnesses~ rise up: they lay to my charge^ things which I don't know about.
12 They reward me evil for good [to] the bereavement of my soul.
13 But as for me, when they were sick my clothing was sackcloth; I chastened my soul with fasting, and my prayer returned to my own bosom:
14 I behaved myself as though [he had been a friend], a brother to me; I bowed down in sadness as one that mourns [for] a mother.
15 But at my halting they rejoiced and gathered together: the slanderers+ gathered themselves together against me, and I didn't know [it]; they tore [me] and didn't cease;
16 with profane^^ jesters for bread, they have gnashed their teeth against me.
17 Lord, how long will you look on? Rescue my soul from their destructions, my only one** from the young lions.
 me; don't let them wink with the eye that hate me without cause.

* or 'soul' ~ Literally 'witnesses of violence' ^ or 'question me about' + or 'base ones'   ^^ or 'hypocritical'   ** see Psalm 22 v20

18 I will give you thanks in the great congregation; I will praise you among the people.
19 Don't let them that are wrongfully~~ my enemies rejoice over
20 For they don't speak peace and they devise deceitful words against the quiet in the land++.
21 And they opened their mouth wide against me; they said, "Aha, aha, our eye has seen [it]".
22 You have seen [it], Jehovah: don't keep silence; o Lord, don't be far from me.
23 Stir yourself up, and awake for my right, for my cause, my God and Lord!
24 Judge me, Jehovah my God, according to your righteousness, and don't let them rejoice over me.
25 Don't let them say in their heart, "Aha, so we would have it" 1. Don't let them say, "We have swallowed him up".
26 Let them be ashamed and brought to confusion together that rejoice at my adversity; let them be clothed with shame and dishonour that magnify themselves against me.
27 Let them exult and rejoice that delight in my righteousness; and let them say continually, "Jehovah be magnified, who delights in the prosperity of his servant".
28 And my tongue shall talk of your righteousness [and] of your praise all the day.

~~ or 'with false pretext'   ++ or 'on the earth'   1 Literally 'our desire'

Psalm 36

To the chief Musician. [A psalm] of the servant of Jehovah; of David

1 The transgression of the wicked utters* within my heart, "There is no fear of God before his eyes".
2 For he flatters himself in his own eyes, [even] when his iniquity is found to be hateful.
3 The words of his mouth are wickedness~ and deceit: he has left off being wise or doing good.
4 He devises wickedness~ upon his bed; he sets himself in a way that is not good: he doesn't abhor evil.
5 Jehovah, your loving-kindness is in the heavens and your faithfulness [reaches] to the clouds.
6 Your righteousness is like the high mountains^; your judgments are a great deep: you, Jehovah, preserve man and beast.
7 How precious is your loving-kindness, o God! So the sons of men take refuge under the shadow of your wings.
8 They shall be abundantly satisfied with the fatness of your house; and you will make them drink of the river of your pleasures+.
9 For with you is the fountain of life: in your light we shall see light.
10 Continue your loving-kindness to them that know you, and your righteousness to the upright in heart;
11 don't let the foot of pride come against me, and don't let the hand of the wicked drive me away.
12 There are the workers of iniquity fallen: they are cast down and are not able to rise.

---

* as an oracle; like 'says' in Genesis 22 v16   ~ or 'vanity', or 'mischief'
^ Literally 'mountains of God' (see Psalms 68 v15, 80 v10)   + plural of Eden

Psalm 37 (acrostic)
[A psalm] of David

1 Don't fret yourself because of evildoers, and don't be envious of those that work unrighteousness;
2 for they shall soon be cut down like the grass, and fade as the green herb.
3 Confide in Jehovah and do good; dwell in the land and feed on* faithfulness;
4 and delight yourself in Jehovah and he will give you the desires of your heart.
5 Commit your way to~ Jehovah and rely upon him: he will bring [it] to pass; and
6 he will bring forth your righteousness as the light and your judgment^ as the noonday.
7 Rest in Jehovah and wait patiently for him: don't fret because of him that prospers in his way, because of him that brings mischievous devices to pass.
8 Cease from anger and forsake wrath;
9 don't fret: it [would be] only to do evil. For evildoers shall be cut off; but those that wait on Jehovah they shall possess the land+.
10 For yet a little while and the wicked is not; and you consider his place but he^^ is not.
11 But the meek shall possess the land and shall delight themselves in the abundance of prosperity**.
12 The wicked plots against the righteous and gnashes his teeth against him.
13 The Lord laughs at him; for he sees that his day is coming.
14 The wicked have drawn out the sword and have bent their bow to cast down the afflicted and needy, to slay those that are upright in [the] way:
15 their sword shall enter into their own heart and their bows shall be broken.
16 The little that the righteous have is better than the abundance of many wicked;
17 for the arms of the wicked shall be broken, but Jehovah upholds~~ the righteous.
18 Jehovah knows the days of the perfect; and their inheritance shall be for ever:
19 they shall not be ashamed in the time of evil, and in the days of

---

* or 'give yourself to'   ~ Literally 'roll your way upon'
^or 'your right'   +or 'the earth' (same in verses 11, 22, 29, 34)
^^ or 'it'   ** or 'peace'   ~~ or 'sustains' (as in Psalm 3 v5)

famine they shall be satisfied.

20 For the wicked shall perish and the enemies of Jehovah shall be as the fat of lambs++: they shall consume, like smoke they shall consume.

21 The wicked borrows and does not pay again; but the righteous is gracious and gives:

22 for those blessed of him shall possess the land and they that are cursed of him shall be cut off.

23 The steps of a man *(geber)* are established by Jehovah and he delights in his way:

24 though he fall, he shall not be utterly cast down for Jehovah upholds his 1 hand.

25 I have been young and now am old, and I have not seen the righteous forsaken nor his seed begging bread:

26 all the day he is gracious and lends, and his seed shall be a blessing.

27 Depart from evil and do good, and dwell for evermore;

28 for Jehovah loves judgment and will not forsake his saints *(chasid)*: they are preserved for ever; but the seed of the wicked shall be cut off.

29 The righteous shall possess the land and dwell in it for ever.

30 The mouth of the wicked proffers wisdom and his tongue speaks judgment:

31 the law of his God is in his heart; his goings shall not slide.

32 The wicked watch the righteous and seeks to slay him:

33 Jehovah will not leave him in his hand nor condemn him when he is judged.

34 Wait for Jehovah and keep his way, and he will exalt you to possess the land: when the wicked are cut off, you shall see [it].

35 I have seen the wicked in great power and spreading like a green tree in its native soil:

36 but he passed away 2 , and behold, he was not: and I sought him but he was not found.

37 Mark the perfect and behold the upright for the end of [that] man is peace 3;

38 but the transgressors shall be destroyed together; the future of the wicked shall be cut off.

39 But the salvation of the righteous is of Jehovah: he is their strength in time of trouble.

40 And Jehovah will help them and deliver them: he will deliver them from the wicked and save them, for they trust in him.

++ others 'the splendour of the meadows'
1 or 'upholds (or 'sustains') [him with] his hand'
2 or 'and one passed by' 3 or 'for there is a future to the man of peace'

Psalm 38

A psalm of David, to bring to remembrance

1 Jehovah, don't rebuke me in your wrath*; neither chasten me in your hot displeasure~.
2 For your arrows stick fast in me, and you hand comes down upon me.
3 There is no soundness in my bones because of your indignation^, no peace in my bones because of my sin.
4 For my iniquities are gone over my head: as a heavy burden they are too heavy for me.
5 My wounds stink, they are corrupt+ because of my foolishness.
6 I am depressed; I am bowed down beyond measure; I go mourning all the day.
7 For my loins are full of burning^^, and there is no soundness in my flesh.
8 I am faint and broken beyond measure; I roar by reason of the agitation of my heart.
9 Lord, all my desire is before you, and my sighing is not hidden from you.
10 My heart throbs, my strength has left me; and the light of my eyes, it is also no more with me.
11 My lovers and my associates stand aloof from my stroke**, and my kinsmen stand afar off.
12 And they that seek after my life lay snares [for me]; and they that seek my hurt speak mischievous things and meditate~~ deceits all the day long.
13 But I, as a deaf [man], don't hear; and am as dumb man that doesn't open his mouth.
14 Yes, I am as a man that doesn't hear, and in whose mouth are no reproofs.
15 For in you, Jehovah, I hope: you will answer, o Lord my God.
16 For I said, "Don't let them rejoice over me! When my foot slipped, they magnified [themselves] against me.
17 For I am ready to halt, and my pain is continually before me.
18 For I will declare my iniquity, I am grieved for my sin.

* means 'indignation' from the idea of 'breaking out into anger'
~ 'heat of anger' is stronger (as in Psalm 88 v7). Wrath and displeasure are words of discipline
^ 'punitive anger against evil' – same word used in Psalms 69 v24, 78v49, 102 v10
+ or 'they run'   ^^ or a loathsome [plague]'   ** or 'plague'   ~~ or 'talk'

19 But my enemies are lively, they are strong; and they that hate me wrongfully are multiplied:
20 and they that render evil for good are adversaries++ to me; because I pursue what is good.
21 Don't forsake me, Jehovah; o my God, don't be far from me.
22 Make haste to help me, o Lord, my salvation.

++ plural of 'Satan' (as in Psalms 71 v13, 109 v4,20,29)

Psalm 39
To the chief Musician, to Jeduthun
A psalm of David

1 I said, "I will take heed to my ways that I don't sin with my tongue: I will keep my mouth with a muzzle while the wicked is before me".
2 I was dumb with silence, I held my peace from good; and my sorrow was stirred.
3 My heart burned within me; the fire was kindled in my musing: I spoke with my tongue.
4 Make me to know, Jehovah, my end and the measure of my days, what it is: I shall know how frail I am.
5 Behold, you have made my days [as] hand-breadths, and my lifetime is as nothing before you; truly, every man, [even] the high placed* is altogether vanity. Selah.
6 Truly man walks in a vain show~; truly they are disquieted in vain^; he heaps up [riches] and does not know who shall gather them.
7 And now, what do I wait for, Lord? My hope is in you.
8 Deliver me from all my transgressions; don't make me the reproach of the foolish.
9 I was dumb, I didn't open my mouth; for you have done [it].
10 Remove your stroke away from me: I am consumed by the blow of your hand.
11 When you with rebukes correct a man for iniquity, you make his beauty to consume away like a moth: surely, every man is vanity. Selah.
12 Hear my prayer, Jehovah, and give ear to my cry; don't be silent at my tears: for I am a stranger with you, a sojourner, like all my fathers.
13 Look away from me and let me recover strength+ before I go hence and be no more.

---

* or 'who stands'   ~ Literally 'in an image (shadow)'
^ or 'for vanity' (as in v5 and 11)   + or 'brighen up'

Psalm 40

To the chief Musician.
Of David. A psalm

1 I waited patiently for Jehovah and he inclined to me and heard my cry.
2 And he brought me up out of the pit of destruction, out of the miry clay, and set my feet upon a rock; he has established my goings;
3 and he has put a new song in my mouth, praise to our God. Many shall see it and shall confide in Jehovah.
4 Blessed is the man *(geber)* that has made Jehovah his confidence and does not turn to the proud and to such as turn aside to lies.
5 You, o Jehovah my God, have multiplied your marvellous works, and your thoughts towards us: they cannot be reckoned up in order to you; if I were to declare and [speak] them, they are more than can be numbered.
6 Sacrifice* and oblation you did not desire: you have prepared~ my ears. Burnt-offering and sin-offering you have not demanded;
7 then I said, "Behold, I come, in the volume^ of the book it is written of me -
8 "to do your good pleasure, my God, is my delight, and your law is within my heart+".
9 I have published right in the great congregation: behold, I have not withheld my lips, Jehovah, you know.
10 I have not hidden your righteousness within my heart; I have declared your faithfulness and your salvation: I have not concealed your loving-kindness and your truth from the great congregation.
11 Don't withhold, Jehovah, your tender mercies from me; let your loving-kindness and your truth continually preserve me.
12 For innumerable evils have encompassed me: my iniquities^^ have taken hold upon me so that I cannot see**; they are more than the hairs of my head, and my heart has failed me.
13 Be pleased, o Jehovah, to deliver me: Jehovah, make haste to help me.
14 Let them be ashamed and brought to confusion together that seek after my soul to destroy it; let them be turned backward and confounded that take pleasure in my adversity;

---

* Hebrew words for the four offerings are: *olah* – burnt-offering; *minchah* – meat-offering; *shelem* – peace-offering; *chataath* – sin-offering
~ Literally 'dug' or 'hollowed out'   ^ or 'roll'
+ Literally 'bowels   ^^ or 'my punishments'   ** or 'look at them'

15 let them be desolate because of their shame, that say to me, "Aha! Aha!"
16 Let all those that seek you be glad and rejoice in you; let such as love your salvation say continually, "Jehovah be magnified!"
17 But I am afflicted and needy: the Lord thinks upon me. You are my help and my deliverer: my God, do not delay~~.

~~ Compare verses 13-17 with Psalm 70

Psalm 41
To the chief Musician. A psalm of David

1 Blessed is he that understands* the poor: Jehovah will deliver him in the day of evil.

2 Jehovah will preserve him and keep him alive; he shall be made happy in the land~; and you will not deliver him to the will of his enemies (tzar).

3 Jehovah will sustain him on the bed of languishing: you turn all his bed in his sickness.

4 As for me, I said, "Jehovah, be gracious to me: heal my soul for I have sinned against you".

5 My enemies wish me evil^: "When will he die, and his name perish?"

6 And if one comes to see [me], he speaks falsehood; his heart gathers wickedness to itself: he goes abroad, he tells [it].

7 All that hate me whisper together against me; against me they devise my hurt+.

8 "A thing of Belial cleaves fast to^^ him, and now that he is laid down, he will rise up no more".

9 Yes, my own familiar friend** in whom I confided, who ate of my bread, has lifted up [his] heel against me.

10 But you, Jehovah, be gracious to me , and raise me up that I may requite them.

11 By this I know that you delight in me because my enemies don't triumph over me.

12 But as for me, you uphold me in my integrity and set me before your face for ever.

‡   ‡   ‡

13 Blessed be Jehovah, the God of Israel, from eternity to eternity! Amen and amen

---

* or 'attends to', 'gives heed to', 'owns'   ~ or 'on the earth'
^ or 'speak evil of me'   + or 'they impute evil to me'   ^^ or 'is poured out upon'
** Literally 'the man *(ish)* of my peace'

SECOND BOOK

Psalm 42
To the chief Musician.
An instruction of* the sons of Korah

1 As the hart pants for the water-brooks, so my soul pants after you, o God.
2 My soul thirsts for God, for the living God: when shall I come and appear before God?
3 My tears have been my bread day and night while they say to me all the day, "Where is your God?"
4 These things I remember and have poured out my soul within me: how I passed along with the multitude, how I went on with them to the house of God, with the voice of joy and praise, a festive multitude.
5 Why are you cast down, my soul, and disquieted in me? Hope in God; for I shall yet praise~ him [for] the health^ of his countenance.
6 My God, my soul is cast down within me; therefore I remember+ you from the land of the Jordan and the Hermons, from Mount Mizar^^.
7 Deep calls to deep at the noise of your cataracts; all your breakers and your billows have gone over me.
8 In the daytime Jehovah will command his loving-kindness, and in the night his song shall be with me, a prayer to the God of my life.
9 I will say to God my rock, "Why have you forgotten me? Why do I go mourning because of the oppression of the enemy?"
10 As with a crushing in my bones my adversaries reproach me while they say to me all the day, "Where is your God?"
11 Why are you cast down, my soul? And why are you disquieted within me? Hope in God; for I shall yet praise him [who is] the health of my countenance and my God.

* or 'for' (same in v11, and Psalm 43 v4,5 and Psalm 44 v8)
~ or 'thank'
^ Literally 'salvations' (same in Psalm 43 v5, Psalm 53 v6, Psalm 116   v13)
+ or 'because I'   ^^ or 'from the little hill'

Psalm 43
To the chief Musician.
Of the sons of Korah. An instruction.

1 Judge me*, o God, and plead my cause against an ungodly~ nation; deliver me from the deceitful and unrighteous man.
2 For you are the God of my strength: why have you cast me off? Why do I go about mourning because of the oppression of the enemy?
3 Send out your light and your truth: they shall lead me, they shall bring me to your holy mount and to your habitations^.
4 Then I will go to the altar of God, to the God of the gladness of my joy: yes, upon the harp I will praise you, o God, my God.
5 Why are you cast down, o my soul, and why are you disquieted within me? Hope in God; for I shall yet praise him [who is] the health of my countenance and my God.

* Often means 'Do me justice'   ~ Hebrew '*goi lo-chasid* a nation not merciful'
^ or 'tabernacles' (same in Psalm 46 v4, 84 v1, 132 v7)

Psalm 44

To the chief Musician.
Of the sons of Korah. An instruction.

1 O God, with our ears have we heard, our fathers have told us, the work* you wrought in their days, in the days of old;
2 you, by your hand, dispossessed the nations but them you planted: you afflicted the peoples *(leummim)* but them you caused to spread out.
3 For not by their own sword did they take possession of the land, neither did their own arm save them; but your right hand, and your arm, and the light of your countenance – because you delighted in them.
4 You yourself~ are my king, o God: command deliverance^ for Jacob.
5 Through you we will push down our adversaries; through your name we will tread them under that rise up against us.
6 For I will not put confidence in my bow, neither shall my sword save me.
7 For you have saved us from our adversaries, and have put them to shame that hate us.
8 In God we will boast all the day, and we will praise your name for ever. Selah.
9 But you have cast off and put us to confusion, and do not go forth with our armies;
10 you have made us to turn back from the adversary, and they that hate us spoil for themselves;
11 you have given us over like sheep [appointed] for meat, and have scattered us among the nations;
12 you have sold your people for nought and have not increased [your wealth] by their price;
13 you make us a reproach to our neighbours, a mockery and a derision for them that are round about us;
14 you make us a byword among the nations, a shaking of the head among the peoples.
15 All the day my confusion is before me, and the shame of my face has covered me,
16 because of the voice of him that reproaches and blasphemes; by reason of the enemy and the avenger+.

---

*   means 'finished work', done with a purpose
~ Literally, 'You, He' or 'You [are] the Same'   ^ Literally 'salvations'
+ as in Psalm 8 v2

17 All this is come upon us; yet we have not forgotten you, neither have we dealt falsely against your covenant:
18 our heart is not turned back, neither have our steps declined from your path;
19 though you have crushed us in the place of jackals, and covered us with the shadow of death.
20 If we had forgotten the name of our God, and stretched out our hands to a strange god,
21 would not God search this out? For he knows the secrets of the heart.
22 But for your sake we are killed all the day long; we are reckoned as sheep for slaughter.
23 Awake, why do you sleep, Lord? Arise, don't cast [us] off for ever.
24 Wherefore do you hide your face [and] forget our affliction and our oppression?
25 For our soul is bowed down to the dust; our belly cleaves to the earth.
26 Rise up for our help, and redeem us for your loving-kindness sake.

Psalm 45

To the chief Musician. Upon Shoshannim.
Of the sons of Korah. An instruction: a song of the beloved.

1 My heart is welling forth [with] a good matter: I say what I have composed* touching the king. My tongue is the pen of a ready writer.
2 You are fairer than the sons of men; grace is poured into your lips: therefore God has blessed you for ever.
3 Gird your sword upon [your] thigh, o mighty one, [in] your majesty and your splendour;
4 and [in] your splendour ride prosperously because of truth and meekness [and] righteousness: and your right hand shall teach you terrible things.
5 Your arrows are sharp – peoples fall under you – in the heart of the king's enemies.
6 Your throne, o God, is for ever and ever; a sceptre of uprightness is the sceptre of your kingdom:
7 you have loved righteousness and hated wickedness; therefore God, your God, has anointed you with the oil of gladness above your companions.
8 Myrrh and aloes, cassia, are all your garments; out of ivory palaces stringed instruments have made you glad~.
9 Kings' daughters are among your honourable women; upon your right hand stands the queen in gold of Ophir.
10 Hearken, daughter, and see, and incline your ear, and forget your own people and your father's house:
11 and the king will desire your beauty; for he is your Lord, and worship him.
12 And the daughter of Tyre with a gift, the rich ones among the people *(ammim)*, shall court your favour.
13 All glorious is the king's daughter within+; her clothing is of wrought gold:
14 she shall be brought to the king in raiment of embroidery; the virgins behind her, her companions, shall be brought in to you:
15 with joy and gladness they shall be brought; they shall enter into the king's palace.
16 Instead of your fathers shall be your sons; you shall make them princes in all the earth *(erets)*.
17 I will make your name to be remembered throughout all generations; therefore the peoples shall praise you^ for ever and ever.

* or 'my occupation'   ~ or 'from which they have gladdened you'
\+ i.e in the royal apartments   ^ or 'give you thanks'

Psalm 46
To the chief Musician. Of the sons of Korah.
On Alamoth. A song

1 God is our refuge and strength, a help in distresses, very readily found.
2 Therefore we will not fear though the earth be removed, and though the mountains be carried into the heart of the seas;
3 though the waters roar [and] foam, though the mountains shake with the swelling. Selah.
4 There is a river whose streams make glad the city of God, the sanctuary of the habitations* of the Most High.
5 God is in the midst of her; she shall not be moved: God shall help her at the dawn of the morning.
6 The nations raged, the kingdoms were moved; he uttered his voice, the earth melted.
7 Jehovah of hosts is with us; the God of Jacob is our high fortress. Selah.
8 Come, behold the works~ of Jehovah, what desolations he has made in the earth;
9 he has made wars to cease to the end of the earth; he breaks the bow and cuts the spear in sunder; he burns the chariots in the fire.
10 "Be still, and know that I am God: I will be exalted in the earth".
11 Jehovah of hosts is with us; the God of Jacob is our high fortress. Selah.

* or 'tabernacles' – see Psalm 43 v3   ~ strictly 'deeds'

Psalm 47
To the chief Musician. Of the sons of Korah. A psalm

1 All peoples *(ammim)*, clap your hands; shout to God with the voice of triumph!
2 For Jehovah, the Most High, is terrible, a great king over all the earth.
3 He subdues the peoples *(leummim)* under us, and the nations under our feet.
4 He has chosen our inheritance for us, the excellency of Jacob whom he loved. Selah.
5 God has gone up amid shouting, Jehovah amid the sound of the trumpet.
6 Sing psalms* of God, sing psalms; sing psalms to our king, sing psalms!
7 For God is the king of all the earth; sing psalms with understanding~.
8 God reigns over the nations; God sits upon the throne of his holiness.
9 The willing-hearted of the peoples *(ammim)* have gathered together [with]^ the people *(ammim)* of the God of Abraham. For to God [belong] the shields+ of the earth: he is greatly exalted.

* as in Psalm 30 v12   ~ or 'for instruction'   ^ or 'are joined to'
+see Hosea 4 v18: where shields mean 'protectors'

Psalm 48

A song. A psalm. Of the sons of Korah

1 Great is jehovah, and greatly to be praised in the city of our God, in the hill of his holiness.
2 Beautiful in elevation, the joy of the whole earth *(erets)*, is mount Zion, [on] the sides of the north, the city of the great king.
3 God is known in her palaces as* a high fortress.
4 For behold, the kings assembled themselves, they passed by together;
5 they saw – so they marvelled; they were troubled, they fled in consternation:
6 trembling took hold upon them there; anguish, as of a woman in travail.
7 With an east wind you have broken the ships of Tarshish.
8 As we have heard, so we have seen, in the city of Jehovah of hosts, in the city of our God: God establishes it for ever. Selah.
9 We have thought, o God, of your loving-kindness in the midst of your temple.
10 According to your name, o God, so is your praise to the ends of the earth: your right hand is full of righteousness.
11 Let mount Zion rejoice, let the daughters of Judah be glad, because of your judgments.
12 Walk about Zion, and go round about her: count her towers;
13 mark well~ her bulwarks, consider her palaces, that you may tell it to the generation following.
14 For this God is our God for ever and ever; he will be our guide until death.

* or 'God is in her palaces'   ~ or 'set your heart on'

Psalm 49
To the chief Musician. Of the sons of Korah. A psalm

1 Hear this, all peoples *(ammim)*; give ear, all inhabitants of the world*:
2 both men of low and men of high degree~, rich and poor alike.
3 My mouth shall speak wisdom+, and the meditation of my heart shall be understanding:
4 I will incline my ear to a parable, I will open my riddle upon the harp.
5 Why should I fear in the days of adversity, [when] the iniquity of my supplanters^ encompasses me? -
6 they depend on their wealth, and boast themselves in the abundance of their riches...
7 None can by any means redeem his brother, nor give to God a ransom for him
8 (for the redemption of their soul is costly, and must be given up for ever)
9 that he should still live perpetually [and] not see corruption^^.
10 For he sees that wise men die; all alike, the fool and the brutish perish, and they leave their wealth to others.
11 Their inward thought is that their houses are for ever, their dwelling-places from generation to generation: they call the lands after their own names**.
12 Nevertheless, man being in honour does not abide: he is like the beasts that perish.
13 This their way is their folly~~, yet they that come after them delight in their sayings. Selah.
14 Like sheep they are laid in Sheol: Death feeds on them; and the upright shall have dominion over them in the morning; and their comeliness shall be for Sheol to consume, so that there is no habitation for them.
15 But God will redeem my soul from the power of Sheol:for he will receive++ me. Selah.
16 Don't be afraid when a man becomes rich, when the glory of his house is increased:
17 for when he dies, he shall carry nothing away; his glory shall not descend after him.
18 Though he blessed his soul in his lifetime – and men will praise you when you do well for yourself -

---

* or 'age' See Psalm 17 v14 ~ Literally 'both sons of Adam and sons of Ish'
+ Literally 'wisdoms' ^ or 'of them who would trip me up' ^^ or 'the pit'
** or 'their names are proclaimed in the lands' ~~ or 'confidence' ++ or 'take'

19 it [1] shall go to the generation of his fathers: they shall never see light.
20 Man that is in honour, and doesn't understand, is like the beasts that perish.

[1] i.e. his soul

Psalm 50

A psalm. Of Asaph

1 God, Elohim-Jehovah*, has spoken, and called the earth from the rising of the sun to its going down.
2 Out of Zion, the perfection of beauty, God has shined forth.
3 Our God will come, and will not keep silence: fire shall devour before him, and it shall be very tempestuous round about him.
4 He will call to the heavens from above, and to the earth, that he may judge his people *(ammim)*:
5 "Gather to me my godly ones, those that have made a covenant with me by~ sacrifice!"
6 And the heavens shall declare his righteousness; for God executes judgment^ himself. Selah.
7 "Hear, my people *(ammim)*, and I will speak; o Israel, and I will testify to you: I am God, your God.
8 "I will not reprove you for your sacrifices, or your burnt-offerings, continually before me;
9 "I will take no bullock out of your house, [nor] he-goats out of your folds:
10 " for every beast of the forest is mine, the cattle upon a thousand hills;
11 "I know all the fowl of the mountains, and the roaming creatures of the field are mine+:
12 "If I were hungry, I would not tell you; for the world *(tebel)* is mine and all its fulness.
13 "Should I eat the flesh of bulls^^, and drink the blood of goats?
14 "Offer** to God thanksgiving, and perform your vows to the Most High;
15 "and call upon me in the day of trouble; I will deliver you, and you shall glorify me".
16 But to the wicked God says, "What have you to do to declare my statutes, or that you should take my covenant into your mouth,
17 seeing you have hated correction~~ and have cast my words behind you?
18 "When you saw a thief, you took pleasure in him, and your portion was with the adulterers;
19 "you let your mouth loose to evil, and your tongue frames deceit;

---

* El Elohim Jehovah ~ strictly 'over' ^ or 'is judge' + or 'before me'
^^ strictly 'the strong ones' ** or 'sacrifice' ~~ or 'instruction'

20 "you sit [and] speak against your brother, your revile++ your own mother's son:
21 "these [things] you have done, and I kept silence: you thought that I was altogether like you: [but] I will reprove you, and set [them] in order before your eyes.
22 "Now consider 1 this, you that forget God, in case I tear in pieces, and there is no deliverer.
23 "Whover offers 2 praise 3 glorifies me; and to him that orders [his] way I will show the salvation of God.

++ or 'slander'   1 or 'understand'
2 Literally, 'sacrifice' as in Deuteronomy 12 v15, Psalm 4 v5
3 or 'thanksgiving'

Psalm 51
To the chief Musician. A psalm of David:
when Nathan the prophet came to him after he had gone in to Bathsheba.

1 Be gracious to me, o God, according to your loving-kindness; according to the abundance of your tender mercies, blot out my transgressions.
2 Wash me fully from my iniquity, and cleanse me from my sin.
3 For I acknowledge my transgressions, and my sin is continually before me.
4 Against you, you only, have I sinned and done what is evil in your sight; that you may be justified when you speak, be clear when you judge.
5 Behold, in iniquity was I brought forth, and in sin did my mother conceive me.
6 Behold, you will have* truth in the inward parts; and in the hidden [part] you will make me to know wisdom.
7 Purge~ me with hyssop and I shall be clean; wash me and I shall be whiter than snow.
8 Make me hear gladness and joy; [that] the bones which you have broken may rejoice.
9 Hide your face from my sins, and blot out all my iniquities.
10 Create in me a clean heart, o God, and renew a steadfast^ spirit within me.
11 Don't cast me away from your presence, and don't take the spirit of your holiness from me.
12 Restore to me the joy of your salvation, and let a willing spirit sustain me+.
13 I will teach transgressors your ways, and sinners shall return to you.
14 Deliver me from blood-guiltiness, o God, God of my salvation: my tongue shall sing aloud of your righteousness.
15 Lord, open my lips, and my mouth shall declare your praise.
16 For you don't desire sacrifice; else I would give it; you have no pleasure in burnt-offering.
17 The sacrifices of God are a broken spirit: you won't despise a broken and a contrite heart, o God.
18 Do good in your good pleasure to Zion; build the walls of Jerusalem.
19 Then you shall have^^ sacrifices of righteousness, burnt-offering and whole burnt-offering; then they shall offer up bullocks on your altar.

* or 'desire' or 'take delight in'   ~ strictly 'purge from sin'   ^ or 'right'
\+ or 'uphold me with a willing (liberal in Psalm 47 v9) spirit'
^^ or 'take delight in' (refer back to verses 6, 16)

Psalm 52
To the chief Musician: an instruction. Of David.
When Doeg the Edomite came and told Saul, and said to him,
"David came to the house of Ahimelech"

1 Why do you boast yourself in evil, mighty man? The loving-kindness of God [abides] continually.*
2 Your tongue devises mischievous things, like a sharp razor, practising~ deceit.
3 You have loved evil rather than good, lying rather than speaking righteousness. Selah.
4 You have loved all devouring words, o deceitful tongue!
5 God shall likewise destroy you for ever; he shall take you away, and pluck you out of [your] tent, and root you out of the land of the living. Selah.
6 The righteous also shall see, and fear, and shall laugh at him, [saying],
7 "Behold the man *(geber)* that didn't make God his strength, but put confidence in the abundance of his riches, [and] strengthened himself in his avarice.
8 But as for me, I am like a green olive-tree in the house of God: I will confide in the loving-kindness of God for ever and ever.
9 I will praise you^ for ever because you have done [it]; and I will wait on your name, before your godly ones, for it is good+.

* Literally 'is all the day'   ~ or 'you practiser of'   ^ or 'give you thanks'
+ or 'and I will wait on your name; because it is good before your godly ones'

Psalm 53
To the chief Musician. On Mahalath: an instruction. Of David

1 The fool *(nabal)* has said in his heart, "There is no God!" They have corrupted themselves, and have done abominable iniquity: there is none that does good.
2 God looked down from the heavens upon the children of men to see if there were any that understood, that sought God.
3 Every one of them has gone back, they have together become corrupt: there is none that does good, not even one.
4 Have the workers of iniquity no knowledge, eating up my people [as] they eat bread? They don't call upon God.
5 There they were in great fear, where no fear was; for God scatters the bones of him that encamps against you. You have put [them] to shame, for God has despised them.
6 Oh that the salvation* of Israel would come out of Zion! When God turns again the captivity of his people, Jacob shall be glad, Israel shall rejoice.

*Literally 'salvations' as in Psalm 42 v5

Psalm 54
To the chief Musician. On stringed instruments: an instruction. Of David. When the Ziphites came, and said to Saul, "Isn't David hiding with us?"

1 O God, by your name save me, and by your strength do me justice.
2 O God, hear my prayer: give ear to the words of my mouth.
3 For strangers have risen up against me, and the violent seek after my life*: they have not set God before them. Selah.
4 Behold, God is my helper; the Lord is among them that uphold my soul.
5 He will requite evil to my enemies: in your truth cut them off.
6 I will freely sacrifice~ to you; I will praise^ your name, o Jehovah, because it is good.
7 For he has delivered me out of all trouble+; and my eye has seen [its] desire upon my enemies.

* Hebrew 'soul' as in Psalm 35 v4 and 38 v12
~ or 'I will sacrifice a freewill offering' ^ or 'thank' + or 'pressure' see Psalm 4 v1

Psalm 55
To the chief Musician. On stringed instruments: an instruction. Of David

1 Give ear to my prayer, o God; and don't hide from my supplication.
2 Attend to me, and answer me: I wander about* in my plaint, and I moan aloud,
3 because of the voice of the enemy; because of the oppression of the wicked~: for they cast iniquity^ upon me, and in anger they persecute me.
4 My heart is writhing within me , and the terrors of death have fallen upon me.
5 Fear and trembling have come upon me, and horror has overwhelmed me.
6 And I said, "Oh that I had wings like a dove!" I would fly away and be at rest;
7 behold, I would flee far away, I would lodge in the wilderness; Selah;
8 I would hasten my escape from the stormy wind, from the tempest.
9 Swallow [them] up, Lord; divide their tongue: for I have seen violence and strife in the city.
10 Day and night they go about it upon the walls of it; and iniquity^ and mischief are in the midst of it.
11 Perversities+ are in the midst of it; and oppression and deceit don't depart from its streets^^.
12 For it is not an enemy that has reproached me – then I could have borne it; neither is it he who hates me that has magnified [himself] against me – then I would have hidden myself from him;
13 but it was you, a man *(enosh)* my equal, my intimate, my familiar friend...
14 we who held sweet intercourse together. To the house of God we walked among the throng.
15 Let death seize upon them, let them go down alive into Sheol. For wickedness is in their dwellings, in their midst.
16 As for me, to God I will call; and Jehovah will save me.
17 Evening and morning, and at noon, I will pray and moan aloud; and he will hear my voice.

---

* or 'am restless' ~ see Psalm 9 v5
^ or 'vanity': it is inwardly devised evil. See psalms 7 v14; 10 v7; 66 v18; 90 v10
+ see Psalm 5 v9   ^^ or 'open places'

18 He has redeemed my soul in peace from the battle against me: for there were many about me.

19 God will hear, and afflict them: he that is seated** of old (Selah) ...because there is no change in them, and they don't fear God.

20 He has put forth his hands against such as are at peace with him; he has profaned his covenant.

21 The milky [words] of his mouth~~ were smooth, but his heart was war; his words were softer than oil, yet they are drawn swords.

22 Cast your burden 1 upon Jehovah and he will sustain you; he will never suffer the righteous to be moved.

23 And you , o God, will bring them down into the pit of destruction: bloody and deceitful men shall not live out half their days. But as for me, I will confide in you.

** or 'that abides'   ~~ or 'the words of his mouth were smooth as butter'
1 or 'the portion assigned to you'

Psalm 56
To the chief Musician. On Jonath-elem-rechokim. Of David.
Michtam: when the Philistines took him in Gath.

1 Be gracious to me, o God; for man *(enosh)* would swallow me up*: all the day long fighting he oppresses me.
2 My enemies would swallow [me] up* all the day long; for they are many that fight against me haughtily.
3 In the day that I am afraid, I will confide in you.
4 In God I will praise his word, in God I put my confidence: I will not fear; what can flesh do to me?
5 All the day long they wrest~ my words; all their thoughts are against me for evil.
6 They gather themselves together, they hide themselves; they mark my steps because they wait for my soul.
7 Shall they escape by iniquity? In anger cast down the peoples, o God.
8 You count^ my wanderings; put my tears into your bottle+: are they not in your book?
9 Then shall my enemies *(tzar)* return backward in the day when I call: this I know, for God is for me.
10 In God I will praise [his] word; in Jehovah I will praise [his] word.
11 In God I have put my confidence: I will not fear; what can man do to me?
12 Your vows are upon me, o God: I will render thanks^^ to you.
13 For you have delivered my soul from death; [won't] you [keep] my feet from falling, that I may walk before God in the light of the living?

* strictly 'pant after me' (like a wild beast thirsting for blood – same in Psalm 5v3)
~ or 'torture'   ^ or 'recount'
+ There is a paronomasia in this verse: *Nod* 'wandering' and *N*o*d* 'bottle' (a leathern sack)
^^ or 'thank-offerings'

Psalm 57

To the chief Musician. 'Destroy not'. Of David.
Michtam: when he fled from Saul in the cave.

1 Be gracious to me, o God, be gracious to me; for my soul takes refuge in you: yes, in the shadow of your wings I take refuge until the calamities have passed over.
2 I will call to God, the Most High; to God that performs* [all] for me.
3 He will send from the heavens and save me; he has covered with reproach he who would swallow me up. Selah. God has sent forth his loving-kindness and his truth.
4 My soul is in the midst of lions; I lie down [among] them that breathe out flames, the sons of men (*Adam*) whose teeth are spears and arrows and their tongue a sharp sword.
5 Be exalted above the heavens, o God; let your glory be above all the earth!
6 They have prepared a net for my steps; my soul was bowed down~: they have dug a pit before me; they have fallen into the midst of it. Selah.
7 My heart is fixed, o God, my heart is fixed: I will sing, yes, I will sing psalms
8 Awake, my glory^; awake, lute and harp: I will wake+ the dawn.
9 I will give you thanks among the peoples, o Lord: I will sing psalms of you among the nations *(leummim)*:
10 for your loving-kindness is great to the heavens, and your truth to the clouds.
11 Be exalted above the heavens, o God; let your glory be above all the earth^^.

* or 'perfects'   ~ or 'they bowed down my soul'
^ see notes Psalm 16 v9
+ or 'awake with'. Also in Psalm 108 v2
^^ See Psalm 108 v1-5

Psalm 58
To the chief Musician. 'Destroy not'. Of David. Michtam

1 Is righteousness indeed silent? Do you speak it? Do you judge with equity, you sons of men?
2 Yes, in heart you work wickedness; you weigh out* the violence of your hands in the earth *(erets)*.
3 The wicked go astray from the womb; they err as soon as they are born, speaking lies.
4 Their poison is like the poison of a serpent: [they are] like the deaf adder which stops her ear;
5 which does not hearken to the voice of enchanters, of one charming ever so wisely.
6 O God, break their teeth in their mouth; break out the great teeth of the young lions, o Jehovah.
7 Let them melt away as waters that flow off; when he aims his arrows, let them be as blunted~:
8 let them be as a snail that melts as it passes away; [like] the untimely birth of a woman, don't let them see the sun.
9 Before your pots feel the thorns, green or burning – they shall be whirled away.
10 The righteous shall rejoice when he sees the vengeance; he shall wash his footsteps in the blood of the wicked:
11 and men shall say, "Truly there is fruit for the righteous; truly there is a God that judges in the earth".

* or 'ponder'   ~ Literally '[the point] be cut off'

Psalm 59

To the chief Musician. 'Destroy not'. Of David.
Michtam: when Saul sent, and they watched the house to kill him.

1 Deliver me from my enemies, o God; secure me on high from those that rise up against me.
2 Deliver me from the workers of iniquity, and save me from men of blood.
3 For behold, they lie in wait for my soul; strong ones are gathered against me: not for my transgression, nor for my sin, o Jehovah.
4 They run and prepare themselves without [my] fault: awake to meet me, and behold.
5 Yes, Jehovah, the God of hosts, the God of Israel, do arise to visit all the nations: don't be gracious to any plotters of iniquity. Selah.
6 They return in the evening; they howl like a dog, and go round about the city:
7 behold, they belch out their mouth; swords are in their lips: for who [they say] hears?
8 But you, Jehovah, will laugh at them; you will have all the nations in derision.
9 Their strength!...I will take heed to you; for God is my high fortress.
10 God, whose loving-kindness* will come to meet me – God shall let me see [my desire] upon my enemies.
11 Don't slay them, in case my people forget; by your power make them wander, and bring them down, o Lord, our shield.
12 [Because of] the sin of their mouth, the word of their lips~, let them even be taken in their pride; and because of cursing and lying which they speak.
13 Make an end in wrath, make an end, so that they are no more; that they may know that God rules in Jacob, to the ends of the earth. Selah.
14 And in the evening they shall return, they shall howl like a dog, and go round about the city.
15 They shall wander about for meat, and stay all night^ if they are not satisfied.
16 But as for me, I will sing of your strength; yes, I will sing aloud of your loving-kindness in the morning; for you have been to me a high fortress, and a refuge+ in the day of my trouble.
17 To you, my strength, I will sing psalms; for God is my high fortress, the God of my mercy.

---

* or 'The God of my mercy' as in verse 17   ~ or '[Because] the sin of their mouth is the word of their lips'   ^ or 'murmur'   + strictly 'place of escape'

Psalm 60

To the chief Musician. On Shushan. Testimony.
Michtam of David: to teach.
When he strove with the Syrians of Mesopotamia
and the Syrians of Zobah, and Joab returned
and smote the Edomites in the valley of salt,
twelve thousand.

1 O God, you have cast us off, you have scattered us, you have been displeased: restore us again.
2 You have made the earth *(erets)* tremble, you have rent it: heal its breaches for it shakes.
3 You have shown your people hard things; you have made us drink the wine of bewilderment.
4 You have given a banner to them that fear you that it may be displayed because of the truth (Selah),
5 that your beloved ones may be delivered. Save with your right hand, and answer me*.
6 God has spoken in his holiness: I will exult, I will divide Shechem and mete out the valley of Succoth.
7 Gilead is mine, and Manasseh is mine, and Ephraim is the strength~ of my head; Judah is my law-giver;
8 Moab is my wash-pot; upon Edom I will cast my sandal; Philistia, shout aloud because of me.
9 Who will bring me into the strong city? Who will lead me into Edom?
10 [Won't] you, o God, who had cast us off and did not go forth with our armies?
11 Give us help from trouble; for vain is man's deliverance.
12 Through our God we shall do valiantly; and he it is that will tread down our adversaries^.

* or 'us'   ~ or 'defence'
^ or oppressors; see also note Psalm 8 v2; compare verses 5-12 with Psalm 108 v6-13

Psalm 61
To the chief Musician. On a stringed instrument. [A psalm] of David

1 Hear, o God, my cry; attend to my prayer.
2 From the ends of the earth *(erets)* I will call to you, when my heart is overwhelmed; you will lead me on to a rock which is too high for me*.
3 For you have been a refuge for me, a strong tower from before the enemy.
4 I will sojourn~ in your tent for ever; I will take refuge~ in the cover of your wings. Selah.
5 For you, o God, have heard my vows; you have given [me] the inheritance of those that fear your name.
6 You will add days to the days of the king: his years shall be as many generations^.
7 He shall abide+ before God for ever: bestow loving-kindness and truth that they may preserve him.
8 So I will sing forth your name for ever, performing my vows from day to day.

* or 'which is higher than I'   ~ or 'Let me sojourn – let me take refuge'
^ Literally 'as generation and generation'   + or 'dwell'

Psalm 62

To the chief Musician. On Jeduthun. A psalm of David.

1 Upon God alone my soul rests peacefully*; from him is my salvation.
2 He only is my rock and my salvation; my high fortress: I shall not be greatly moved.
3 How long will you assail a man; will you [seek], all of you, to break him down as a bowing wall or a tottering fence?
4 They only consult to thrust [him] down from his excellency; they delight in lies; they bless with their mouths but in their inward part they curse. Selah.
5 Upon God alone, o my soul, rest peacefully*; for my expectation is from him.
6 He only is my rock and my salvation; my high fortress: I shall not be moved.
7 With God is my salvation and my glory; the rock of my strength, my refuge is in God.
8 Confide in him at all times, people: pour out your heart before him: God is our refuge. Selah.
9 Men of low degree~ are only vanity^; men of high degree~ a lie: laid up in the balance, they go up together [lighter] than vanity^.
10 Don't put confidence in oppression, and don't become vain in robbery; if wealth increases, don't set your heart upon it.
11 Once God has spoken, twice I have heard this, that strength [belongs] to God.
12 And to you, o Lord, [belongs] loving-kindness; for you render to every man according to his work.

* or 'wait(s) in silence'
~ Psalm 49 v2 note: sons (men) of Adam and sons (men) of Ish
^ See Psalm 39 v5,6,11

Psalm 63

A psalm of David; when he was in the wilderness of Judah

1 O God, you are my God: I will seek you early. My soul thirsts for you, my flesh languishes for you in a dry and weary land without water:
2 to see your power and your glory, as I have beheld you in the sanctuary;
3 for your loving-kindness is better than life: my lips shall praise you.
4 So I will bless you while I live; I will lift up my hands in your name.
5 My soul is satisfied as with marrow and fatness, and my mouth shall praise [you] with joyful lips.
6 When I remember you upon my bed, I meditate on you in the night-watches:
7 for you have been my help, and in the shadow of your wings I will sing for joy.
8 My soul follows hard after you: your right hand upholds me.
9 But those that seek my soul, to destroy [it], shall go into the lower parts of the earth;
10 they shall be given over to the power of the sword; they shall be the portion of foxes.
11 But the king shall rejoice in God; every one that swears by him shall glory: for the mouth of them that speak lies shall be stopped.

Psalm 64
To the chief Musician. A psalm of David

1 Hear, o God, my voice in my plaint; preserve my life from fear of the enemy.
2 Hide me from the secret counsel of evildoers, from the tumultuous crowd of the workers of iniquity.
3 who have sharpened their tongue like a sword, [and] have aimed their arrow, a bitter word;
4 that they may shoot in secret* at the perfect: suddenly they shoot at him and don't fear.
5 They encourage themselves in an evil matter, they concert to hide snares; they say, "Who will see them?"
6 They devise iniquities: "We have it ready, the plan is diligently sought out". And each one's inward [thought] and heart is deep.
7 But God will shoot an arrow at them: suddenly they are wounded;
8 by their own tongue they are made to fall over one another: all that see them shall flee away.
9 And all men shall fear, and shall declare God's doing; and they shall wisely consider his work.
10 The righteous shall rejoice in Jehovah, and trust in him; and all the upright in heart shall glory.

* or 'from their hiding-places'

Psalm 65
To the chief Musician. A psalm of David: a song

1 Praise waits for you in silence, o God, in Zion; and to you the vow shall be performed.
2 O you that hears prayer, to you all flesh shall come.
3 Iniquities have prevailed against me: our transgressions, you will forgive* them.
4 Blessed is he who you choose and cause to approach: he shall dwell in your courts. We shall be satisfied with the goodness of your house, of your holy temple~.
5 By terrible things in righteousness you will answer us, o God of our salvation, you, the confidence of all the ends of the earth and of the distant regions of the sea...
6 who by his strength established the mountains, being girded with power;
7 who stills the raging of the seas, the raging of their waves, and the tumult of the peoples *(leummim)*.
8 And they that dwell in the uttermost parts are afraid at your tokens^; you make the outgoings of the morning and evening to rejoice.
9 You have visited the earth *(erets)*, you have watered it+; you greatly enrich it: the river of God is full of water; you provide their^^ corn when you have so prepared it**:
10 you satiate its furrows, you smooth its clods, you make it soft with showers; you bless its springing.
11 You crown the year with your goodness, and your paths drop fatness:
12 they drop upon the pastures of the wilderness, and the hills are girded with gladness.
13 The meadows are clothed with flocks, and the valleys are covered over with corn; they shout for joy, yes, they sing.

* Literally 'make atonement'   ~ or 'the temple of your holiness'
^ or 'signs'   + or 'made it overflow'   ^^ that is, of men
** that is, the earth

Psalm 66
To the chief Musician. A song: a psalm

1 Shout aloud to God, all the earth:
2 sing forth the glory of his name, make his praise glorious;
3 say to God, "How terrible are your works! Because of the greatness of your strength, your enemies come cringing to you.
4 "All the earth shall worship you, and sing psalms to you: they shall sing forth your name". Selah.
5 Come and see the works* of God: he is terrible in [his] doings toward the children of men.
6 He turned the sea into dry [land]; they went through the river on foot: there we rejoiced in him.
7 He rules by his power for ever; his eyes observe the nations: don't exult yourselves, you rebellious. Selah.
8 Bless our God, you peoples *(ammim),* and make the voice of his praise to be heard;
9 who has set our soul in life, and doesn't suffer our feet to be moved.
10 For you, o God, have proved us: you have tried~ us as silver is tried~.
11 You brought us into a net, you laid a heavy burden upon our loins;
12 you caused men to ride over our head; we went through fire and through water: but you have brought us out into abundance^.
13 I will go into your house with burnt-offerings; I will perform my vows to you,
14 which my lips have uttered and my mouth has spoken when I was in trouble.
15 I will offer up to you burnt-offerings of fatted beasts, with the incense of rams; I will offer bullocks with goats. Selah.
16 Come, hear, all you that fear God, and I will declare what he has done for my soul.
17 I called to him with my mouth, and he was extolled with my tongue.
18 Had I regarded iniquity in my heart, the Lord would not hear.
19 But God has heard; he has attended to the voice of my prayer.
20 Blessed be God who has not turned away my prayer, nor his loving-kindness from me!

* or 'deeds'. See Psalm 46 v8   ~ or 'refined' – see Psalms 12 v6, 18 v30
^ same word in Psalm 23 v5 'runs over', 'overflows'

Psalm 67
To the chief Musician. On stringed instruments. A psalm: a song.

1 God be gracious to us, and bless us, [and] cause his face to shine upon* us; Selah,
2 that your way may be known upon earth, your salvation among all nations.
3 Let the peoples *(ammim)* praise you, o God, let all the peoples *(ammim)* praise you.
4 Let the nations *(leummim)* rejoice and sing for joy: for you will judge the peoples *(ammim)* equitably; and the nations *(leummim)* upon earth, you will guide them. Selah.
5 Let the peoples *(ammim)* praise you, o God; let all the peoples *(ammim)* praise you.
6 The earth will yield her increase; God, our God, will bless us;
7 God will bless us and all the ends of the earth shall fear him.

* Literally 'with'

Psalm 68
To the chief Musician. Of David. A psalm: a song.

1 Let God arise, let his enemies be scattered, and let them that hate him flee before him*.
2 As smoke is driven, you will drive them away; as wax melts before the fire, the wicked shall perish at the presence of God.
3 But the righteous shall rejoice: they shall exult before God and be glad with joy.
4 Sing to God, sing forth his name: cast up a way for~ him that rides in the deserts: his name is Jah^; and rejoice before him.
5 A father of the fatherless, and a judge of the widows, is God in his holy habitation.
6 God makes the solitary into families+; those that were bound^^ he brings out into prosperity: but the rebellious dwell in a parched [land].
7 O God, when you went forth before your people, when you marched through the wilderness – (Selah) -
8 the earth trembled, the heavens also dropped at the presence of God, yon Sinai, at the presence of God, the God of Israel**.
9 You, o God, poured a plentiful rain~~ upon your inheritance, and when it was weary you strengthened it.
10 Your flock++ has dwelt there: you have prepared for the afflicted, in your goodness, o God.
11 The Lord gives the word *(omer)*: great is the host of publishers 1.
12 Kings of armies flee; they flee, and she that tarries at home divides the spoil.
13 Though you have lain among the sheepfolds 2, [you shall be as] wings of a dove covered with silver and her feathers with green gold 3.
14 When the Almighty scattered kings in it 4, it became snow-white as Zalmon.
15 [As] mount Bashan is the mount of God 5, a many-peaked mountain [as] mount Bashan.
16 Why do you look with envy, you many-peaked mountains, upon the mount that God has desired for his abode? Yes, Jehovah will dwell [there] for ever.

---

* Similar to something Moses is recorded as saying in Numbers 10 v35
~ or 'triumph in'
^ The existing One, objectively: Jah occurs 43 times from Psalms 68-150
+ or 'makes the solitary to dwell in a home'   ^^ or 'prisoners'
** similar to words in Deborah's song in Judges 5 v3,5   ~~ or 'a rain of free gifts'
++ or 'living assembly'   1 that is women publishing victory. The word is feminine
2 others translate 'pots' or 'ash-grates'   3 strictly 'greenish-yellow
4 i.e. the land   5 or 'A mount of God is mount Bashan'

17 The chariots of God are twenty thousand, thousands upon thousands; the Lord is among them: it is a Sinai in holiness.
18 You have ascended on high, you have led captivity captive: you have received gifts in Man 6, and even [for] the rebellious, for the dwelling 7 [there] of Jah Elohim.
19 Blessed be the Lord: day by day he loads us [with good], the God who is our salvation. Selah.
20 Our God is the God of salvation 8; and with Jehovah, the Lord, are the goings forth [even] from death.
21 Truly God will smite the head of his enemies, the hairy scalp of him that goes on still in his trespasses.
22 The Lord said, "I will bring again from Bashan, I will bring [them] again from the depth of the sea;
23 that you may dip your foot in blood: the tongue of your dogs has its portion from enemies".
24 They have seen your goings, o God, the goings of my God, my king, in the sanctuary.
25 The singers went before, the players on stringed instruments after, in the midst of maidens playing on tabrets.
26 In the congregations bless God, the Lord – those of [you] from the fountain of Israel.
27 There is little Benjamin, their ruler; the princes of Judah, their company; the princes of Zebulun, the princes of Naphtali.
28 Your God has commanded your strength: strengthen, o God, that which you have wrought for us.
29 Because of your temple at Jerusalem kings shall bring presents to you.
30 Rebuke the beast of the reeds, the assembly of the strong, with the calves of the peoples: [every one] submits himself with pieces of silver. Scatter the peoples that delight in war.
31 Great ones shall come out of Egypt: Ethiopia shall quickly stretch out her hands to God.
32 You kingdoms of the earth, sing to God; sing psalms of the Lord (Selah),
33 of him that rides on the heavens, the heavens which are of old 9: there 10, he utters his voice, a mighty voice.
34 Ascribe strength to God: his excellency is over Israel and his strength is in the clouds.
35 You are terrible, o God, out of your sanctuaries – the God of Israel! It is he that gives strength and might to the people. Blessed be God!

6 that is, as man *(Adam)* in connection with mankind   7 see Exodus 25 v8
8 or 'God is for us a God of salvations'   9 Refer to Deuteronomy 33 v27
10 my preference: 'there' for 'lo

Psalm 69

To the chief Musician. Upon Shoshannim. [A psalm] of David

1 Save me, o God, for the waters have come in to [my] soul.
2 I sink in deep mire where there is no standing; I have come into the depths of waters and the flood overflows me.
3 I am weary with my crying, my throat is parched; my eyes fail while I wait for my God.
4 They that hate me without a cause are more than the hairs of my head; they that would destroy me, wrongfully being my enemies, are mighty: then I restored that which I didn't take away.
5 You, o God, know my foolishness, and my trespasses are not hidden from you.
6 Those who wait on you, Lord, Jehovah of hosts, don't let them be ashamed through me; don't let those that seek you be confounded through me, o God of Israel.
7 Because for your sake I have borne reproach; confusion has covered my face.
8 I have become a stranger to my brothers, and an alien to my mother's sons;
9 for the zeal of your house has devoured me, and the reproaches of them that reproach you have fallen upon me.
10 And I wept, my soul was fasting: that also was to my reproach -
11 and I made sackcloth my garment: then I became a proverb to them.
12 They that sit in the gate talk of me, and [I am] the song of the drunkards*.
13 But as for me, my prayer is to you, Jehovah, in an acceptable time: o God, in the abundance of your loving-kindness answer me according to the truth of your salvation:
14 deliver me out of the mire, don't let me sink; let me be delivered from them that hate me and out of the depths of waters.
15 Don't let the flood of waters overflow me, neither let the deep swallow me up; and don't let the pit shut its mouth upon me.
16 Answer me, o Jehovah; for your loving-kindness is good: according to the abundance of your tender mercies, turn toward me;
17 and don't hide your face from your servant for I am in trouble: answer me speedily.
18 Draw near to my soul, be its redeemer~; ransom me because of my enemies.

* Literally 'drinkers of strong drink'
~ see description of redeemer in Leviticus 25 v25; the word can also be 'avenger'

19 You know my reproach and my shame, and my dishonour: my adversaries *(tzar)* are all before you.
20 Reproach has broken my heart, and I am overwhelmed: and I looked for sympathy but there was none; and for comforters but I found none.
21 Yes, they gave me gall^ for my food, and in my thirst they gave me vinegar to drink.
22 Let their table become a snare before them, and their very welfare a trap;
23 let their eyes be darkened so that they don't see, and make their loins continually shake.
24 Pour out your indignation upon them, and let the fierceness of your anger take hold of them.
25 Let their habitation be desolate; let there be no dweller in their tents.
26 For they persecute him whom you have smitten, and they talk for sorrow+ of those whom you have wounded.
27 Add iniquity to their iniquity, and don't let them come into your righteousness.
28 Let them be blotted out of the book of life, and not be written with the righteous.
29 But I am afflicted and sorrowful: let your salvation, o God, set me secure on high.
30 I will praise the name of God with a song, and will magnify him with thanksgiving;
31 and it shall please Jehovah more than an ox – a bullock with horns and cloven hoofs.
32 The meek shall see it, they shall be glad; you that seek God, your heart shall live.
33 For Jehovah hears the needy, and doesn't despise his prisoners.
34 Let the heavens and earth praise him: the seas, and everything that moves in them.
35 For God will save Zion and will build the cities of Judah; and they shall dwell there and possess it:
36 and the seed of his servants shall inherit it, and they that love his name shall dwell there.

^ a bitter and possibly poisonous plant. Gall is referenced in Jeremiah: 8 v14, 23 v15
+ or 'talk of

Psalm 70

To the chief Musician. [A psalm] of David: to bring to remembrance

1 Make haste, o God, to deliver me; Jehovah, [hasten] to my help.
2 Let them be ashamed and brought to confusion that seek after my soul; let them be turned backward and confounded that take pleasure in my adversity;
3 let them turn back because of* their shame that say, "Aha! Aha!"
4 Let those that seek you be glad and rejoice in you, and let such as love your salvation say continually, "Let God be magnified!"
5 But I am afflicted and needy: make haste to me, o God. You are my help and my deliverer: o Jehovah, don't delay.

* or 'for a reward of'

Psalm 71

1 In you, Jehovah, I trust: let me never be ashamed.

2 Deliver me in your righteousness and rescue me; incline your ear to me and save me.

3 Be to me a rock of habitation to which I may continually resort: you have given commandment to save me; for you are my rock* and my fortress.

4 My God, rescue me out of the hand of the wicked, out of the hand of the unrighteous and cruel man.

5 For you are my hope, o Lord Jehovah, my confidence from my youth.

6 On you I have been stayed from the womb; from the bowels of my mother you drew me forth~: my praise shall be continually of you.

7 I have been as a wonder to many; but you are my strong refuge.

8 My mouth shall^ be filled with your praise, with your glory, all the day.

9 Don't cast me off in the time of old age; don't forsake me when my strength fails.

10 For my enemies speak against me, and they that watch for my soul consult together,

11 saying, "God has forsaken him; pursue and seize him, for there is none to deliver".

12 O God, don't be far from me; my God, hasten to my help.

13 Let them be ashamed, let them be consumed, that are adversaries+ to my soul; let them be covered with reproach and dishonour that seek my hurt.

14 But as for me, I will hope continually, and will praise you yet more and more.

15 My mouth shall declare your righteousness, [and] your salvation all the day: for I know not the numbers [thereof].

16 I will go in the might of the Lord Jehovah: I will recall^^ your righteousness, yours alone.

17 O God, you have taught me from my youth, and hitherto I have proclaimed your marvellous works.

18 now also, when I am old and greyheaded, o God, don't forsake me, until I have proclaimed your arm to [this] generation, your might to every one that is to come.

---

* same word as in psalm 18 v2, psalm 31 v3 etc *sela* meaning a high rock
~ or 'are my benefactor'   ^ or 'Let my mouth'   + *Satan* – see Psalm 38 v20
^^ or 'make mention of'

19 And your righteousness, o God, reaches on high**, you who have done great things: o God, who is like you?
20 You, who has shown us many and sore troubles, will revive us again, and will bring us up again from the depths of the earth;
21 you will increase my greatness and comfort me on every side~~.
22 I will also praise you++ with the psaltery 1, even your truth, my God; to you I will sing psalms with the harp, o holy One of Israel.
23 My lips shall exult when I 2 sing psalms to you; and my soul which you have redeemed.
24 My tongue also shall talk of your righteousness all the day; for they shall be ashamed, for they shall be brought to confusion, that seek my hurt.

** or 'is very high'   ~~ or 'and turn and comfort me'++ or 'give you thanks'
1 Literally 'an instrument, a lute'   2 or 'exult; for I will'

Psalm 72
For* Solomon

1 O God, give the king your judgments, and your righteousness to the king's son.
2 He will judge your people with righteousness and your afflicted with judgment~.
3 The mountains shall bring peace to the people, and the hills, by righteousness.
4 He will do justice to the afflicted of the people; he will save the children of the needy, and will break in pieces the oppressor.
5 They shall fear you as long as sun and moon endure^, from generation to generation+.
6 He shall come down like rain on the mown grass, as showers that water the earth *(erets)*.
7 In his days the righteous shall flourish, and abundance of peace till the moon be no more.
8 And he shall have dominion from sea to sea, and from the river to the ends of the earth *(erets)*.
9 The dwellers in the desert shall bow before him, and his enemies shall lick the dust.
10 The kings of Tarshish and of the isles shall render presents^^; the kings of Sheba and Seba shall offer tribute:
11 yes, all kings shall bow before him; all nations shall serve him.
12 For he will deliver the needy who cries, and the afflicted, who has ** no helper.
13 He will have compassion on the poor and needy, and will save the souls of the needy;
14 he will redeem their souls from oppression and violence, and precious shall their blood be in his sight.
15 And he shall live; and to him shall be given of the gold of Sheba; and prayer shall be made for him continually: all the day he shall be blessed.
16 There shall be abundance~~ of corn in the earth, upon the top of the mountains; the fruit of it shall shake like Lebanon; and they of the city shall bloom like the herb of the earth.
17 His name shall endure for ever; his name shall be continued as long as the sun: and [men] shall bless themselves in him; all nations shall call him blessed.

‡ ‡ ‡

* or 'of' or 'concerning' ~ or 'rectitude'
^ Literally 'with the sun and before the moon'   + or 'generation of generations'
^^ or 'shall present gifts' ** or 'him that has' ~~ or 'handfuls'

18 Blessed be Jehovah Elohim, the God of Israel, who alone does wondrous things!
19 And blessed be his glorious name for ever! And let the whole earth be filled with his glory! Amen, and amen.
20 The prayers of David, the son of Jesse, are ended.

THIRD BOOK

Psalm 73
A psalm of Asaph

1 Truly God is good to Israel, to such as are of a pure heart.
2 But as for me, my feet were almost gone, my steps had well nigh slipped;
3 for I was envious at the arrogant, seeing the prosperity of the wicked.
4 For they have no pangs in their death, and their body* is well nourished;
5 they don't have the hardships of mankind~, neither are they plagued like [other] men:
6 therefore pride encompasses them as a neck-chain, violence covers them [as] a garment;
7 their eyes stand out from fatness, they exceed the imaginations of their heart:
8 they mock and speak wickedly of oppression, they speak loftily:
9 they set their mouth in the heavens, and their tongue walks through the earth.
10 Therefore his people turn hither and waters in fulness are wrung out to them.
11 And they say, "How can God know, and is there knowledge in the Most High?"
12 Behold, these are the wicked, and they prosper in the world^: they heap up riches.
13 Truly I have purified my heart in vain and washed my hands in innocency:
14 for all day long I have been plagued, and chastened every morning.
15 If I said, "I will speak thus", I should be faithless to the generation of your children.
16 When I thought to be able to know this, it was a grievous task+ in my eyes;
17 until I went into the sanctuaries of God; [then] I^^ understood their end.
18 Truly you set them in slippery places, you cast them down in ruins.

---

* or 'strength'   ~ *Enosh* as in Psalm 8 v4
^ or 'and they are ever at rest' (i.e. careless)
+ 'labour' or 'trouble' or 'hardships' (as v5)   ^^ or '[and] I had considered'

19 How they are suddenly made desolate! They pass away, consumed with terrors.
20 As a dream, when one awakes, Lord, on arising**, you will despise their image.
21 When my heart was a ferment, and I was pricked in my reins,
22 then I was brutish and knew nothing; I was [as] a beast with you.
23 Nevertheless I am continually with you: you have held my right hand;
24 you will guide me by your counsel, and after the glory you will receive me.
25 Whom have I in the heavens? And there is none upon earth I desire beside you.
26 My flesh and my heart fails: God is the rock of my heart and my portion for ever.
27 For behold, they that are far from you shall perish; you destroy every one that goes a whoring~~ from you.
28 But as for me, it is good for me to draw near to God: I have put my trust in the Lord Jehovah, that I may declare all your works 1.

** or 'in wrath'   ~~ in other versions 'who is unfaithful to you'
1 'Things made' 'wrought' as in Genesis 2 v2

Psalm 74
An instruction: of Asaph

1 Why, o God, have you cast us off for ever? [Why] does your anger smoke against the sheep of your pasture?
2 Remember your assembly, which you have purchased of old, which you have redeemed* [to be] the portion~ of your inheritance, this Mount Zion wherein you have dwelt.
3 Lift up your steps to the perpetual desolations: everything in the sanctuary the enemy has destroyed.
4 Your adversaries *(tzar)* roar in the midst of your place of assembly; they set up their signs [for] signs^.
5 [A man] was known as he could lift up axes in the thicket of trees;
6 and now they break down its carved work altogether, with hatchets and hammers.
7 They have set your sanctuary on fire, they have profaned the habitation+ of your name to the ground.
8 They said in their heart, "Let us destroy^^ them together". They have burned up all God's places of assembly in the land.
9 We don't see our signs; there isn't any prophet any more, neither is there any among us that knows how long.
10 How long, o God, shall the adversary reproach? Shall the enemy contemn your name for ever?
11 Why do you withdraw your hand, and your right hand? [Pluck it] out of your bosom: consume [them].
12 But God is my king of old, accomplishing deliverances in the midst of the earth.
13 You divided the sea by your strength; you broke the heads of the monsters on the waters;
14 you broke in pieces the heads of leviathan**, you gave him to be meat to those that people the desert.
15 You split~~ fountain and torrent, you dried up ever-flowing rivers.
16 The day is yours, the night also is yours; you have prepared the moon++ and the sun:
17 you have set all the borders of the earth; summer and winter –

---

* As in Psalm 69 v18   ~ Literally 'staff [for measuring]' or 'tribe'
^ See Exodus 4 v17 (Moses used his staff to show God's signs) and 10 v2
+ Hebrew is *mishkan*, used for 'tabernacle' in Exodus 26 v1 etc, and 'dwells ' in Psalm 26 v8   ^^ or 'oppress' ** as in Job 3 v8 and 41 v1: seems it could be 'the crocodile'   ~~ Darby translates this 'you did cleave'
++ or 'light-bearer' that is, what gives light per Genesis 1 v14-16 and Exodus 25 v6

you formed them.
18 Remember this, than an enemy has reproached Jehovah, and a foolish 1 people has contemned your name.
19 Don't give up the soul of your turtle-dove to the wild beast 2; don't forget the troop 3 of your afflicted for ever.
20 Have respect to the covenant; for the dark places of the earth are full of the dwellings of violence.
21 Oh don't let the oppressed one return ashamed; let the afflicted and needy praise your name.
22 Rise up, o God, plead your own cause: remember how the foolish man reproaches you all the day;
23 don't forget the voice of your adversaries: the tumult of those that rise up against you ascends continually.

1 or 'vile' 'impious' – see also verse 22 and Psalm 53 v1
2 or 'Don't give up your turtle-dove to the greedy troop' (or 'herd')
3 others 'life' as 'flock' (Psalm 68 v10)

Psalm 75

To the chief Musician. 'Destroy not'. A psalm of Asaph: a song.

1 We give thanks to you, o God, we give thanks; and your name is near: your marvellous works declare it.
2 When I shall receive the assembly*, I will judge with equity.
3 The earth *(erets)* and all its inhabitants are dissolved: I have established its pillars. Selah.
4 I said to the wicked, "Don't boast"; and to the wicked, "Don't lift up the horn:
5 "don't lift up your horn on high; don't speak arrogantly with a stiff neck".
6 For it's not from the east or from the west, nor yet from the south, that exaltation [comes]:
7 For God is the judge; he puts down one and exalts another.
8 For in the hand of Jehovah there is a cup, and it foams~ with wine, it is full of mixture; and he pours out of the same; yes, all the wicked of the earth shall drain off its dregs [and] drink.
9 But as for me, I will declare for ever; I will sing psalms to the God of Jacob.
10 And all the horns of the wicked I will cut off; [but] the horns of the righteous shall be exalted.

* or 'When I shall reach (seize) the set time' – see Leviticus 23 v2
~ or 'it is red'

Psalm 76
To the chief Musician. On stringed instruments.
A psalm of Asaph: a song.

1 In Judah God is known, his name is great in Israel;
2 and in Salem is his tent*, and his dwelling-place in Zion.
3 There he broke the flashings of the bow, shield and sword and battle. Selah.
4 More glorious are you, more excellent, than the mountains of prey.
5 The stout-hearted are made a spoil, they have slept their sleep; and none of the men of might have found their hands.
6 At your rebuke, o God of Jacob, both chariot and horse are cast into a dead sleep.
7 You, you are to be feared, and who can stand before you once you are angry?
8 You caused judgment to be heard from the heavens; the earth *(erets)* feared and was still,
9 when God rose up to judgment, to save all the meek of the earth *(erets)*. Selah.
10 For the fury of man shall praise you; the remainder of fury you will gird on yourself~.
11 Vow and pay to Jehovah your God: let all that are round about him bring presents to him that is to be feared.
12 He cuts off the spirit of princes; [he] is terrible to the kings of the earth.

* or 'booth'   ~ or 'restrain'

Psalm 77
To the chief Musician. On Jeduthun. Of Asaph. A psalm.

1 My voice is to God, and I will cry; my voice is to God, and he will give ear to me.
2 In the day of my trouble, I sought the Lord; my hand was stretched out* in the night, and didn't slack; my soul refused to be comforted.
3 I remembered God, and I moaned; I complained, and my spirit was overwhelmed. Selah.
4 You hold my eyelids open; I am full of disquiet and cannot speak.
5 I consider the days of old, the years of ancient times.
6 I remember my song in the night; I muse in my own heart, and my spirit makes a diligent search.
7 Will the Lord cast off for ever? And will he be favourable no more?
8 Has his loving-kindness ceased for ever? Has [his] word *(omer)* come to an end from generation to generation?
9 Has God forgotten to be gracious? Or has he in anger shut up his tender mercies? Selah.
10 Then I said, "This is my weakness: - the years of the Most High
11 "I will remember – the works~ of Jah"; for I will remember your works of old,
12 and I will meditate upon all your work, and muse upon your doings.
13 O God, your way is in the sanctuary: who is so great a god as God?
14 You are the God that does wonders; you have declared your strength amongst the peoples.
15 You have redeemed with [your] arm your people, the sons of Jacob and Joseph. Selah.
16 The waters saw you, o God, the waters saw you; they trembled, yes, the depths were troubled:
17 the thick clouds poured out water; the skies sent out a sound, yes, your arrows went abroad:
18 the voice of your thunder was in the whirlwind, lightnings lit up the world; the earth was troubled and it quaked.
19 Your way is in the sea, and your paths are in the great waters; and your footsteps are not known.
20 You led your people like a flock by the hand of Moses and Aaron.

---

* or 'was poured out' or 'my sore ran'   ~ strictly 'doings', 'exploits'; in verse 12 'doings' is more like 'actions. In verse 12 'work' is 'a thing done' as in Isaiah 45 v9

Psalm 78
An instruction. Of Asaph

1 Give ear, o my people, to my law; incline your ears to the words of my mouth.
2 I will open my mouth in a parable; I will utter* riddles from of old,
3 which we have heard and known, and our fathers have told us:
4 we will not hide [them] from their sons, showing forth to the generation to come the praises of Jehovah, and his strength, and his marvellous works which he has done.
5 For he established a testimony in Jacob, and appointed a law in Israel, which he commanded our fathers, that they should make them known to their children;
6 that the generation to come might know [them], the children that should be born: that they might rise up and tell [them] to their children,
7 and that they might set their hope in God, and not forget the works~ of God, but observe his commandments;
8 and might not be as their fathers, a stubborn and rebellious generation, a generation that didn't prepare their heart and whose spirit was not steadfast with God.
9 The sons of Ephraim, armed bowmen, turned back in the day of battle.
10 They didn't keep the covenant of God and refused to walk in his law;
11 and forgot his doings, and his marvellous works which he had shown them:
12 in the sight of their fathers he had done wonders, in the land of Egypt, the field of Zoan^.
13 He clave the sea and caused them to pass through; and made the waters to stand as a heap;
14 and he led them with a cloud in the daytime and all the night with the light of fire.
15 He clave rocks in the wilderness and gave [them] drink as out of the depths, abundantly;
16 and he brought streams out of the rock+, and caused waters to run down like rivers.
17 Yet they still went on sinning against him, provoking^^ the Most High in the desert:

* As in Psalm 19 v2   ~ As in Psalm 77 v11   ^ that is Tanis, a town in lower Egypt+ *sela* as in Psalm 31 v3   ^^ or 'rebelling against'

18 and they tempted God in their heart, by asking meat for their lust;
19 and they spoke against God: they said, "Is God able to prepare** a table in the wilderness?
20 "Behold, he smote the rock and waters gushed out and streams overflowed; is he able to give bread also, or provide flesh for his people?"
21 Therefore Jehovah heard and was wroth; and fire was kindled against Jacob, and anger also went up against Israel:
22 because they didn't believe in God, and didn't confide in his salvation;
23 though he had commanded the clouds from above and had opened the doors of the heavens,
24 and had rained down manna upon them to eat, and had given them the corn of the heavens.
25 Man did eat the bread of the mighty; he sent them provision to the full.
26 he caused the east wind to rise in the heavens, and by his strength he brought the south wind;
27 and he rained down flesh upon them as dust, and feathered fowl as the sand of the seas,
28 and he let it fall in the midst of their camp, round about their habitations:
29 and they ate and were well filled; for what they lusted after he brought to them.
30 They were not alienated from their lust, their meat was yet in their mouths
31 when the anger of God went up against them; and he slew the fattest of them and smote down the chosen men of Israel.
32 For all this, they sinned still, and didn't believe in~~ his marvellous works;
33 and he consumed their days in vanity and their years in terror.
34 When he slew them, then they sought him and returned and sought early after God;
35 and they remembered that God was their rock, and God, the Most High, their redeemer++.
36 But they flattered 1 him with their mouth, and lied to him with their tongue;
37 for their heart was not firm toward him, neither were they steadfast in his covenant.
 away and does not come again.

** or 'furnish' as in Proverbs 9 v2   ~~ or 'by'   ++ as in Psalm 69 v18
1 meaning 'make pretence', other places 'entice' or 'deceive'

38 But he was merciful: he forgave the iniquity and didn't destroy [them]; but many a time he turned his anger away and didn't stir up all his fury:
39 and he remembered that they were flesh, a breath that passes
40 How often they provoked him in the wilderness and grieved him in the desert!
41 And they turned again and tempted God and grieved 2 the Holy One of Israel.
42 They didn't remember his hand, the day when he delivered them from the oppressor,
43 how he set his signs in Egypt and his miracles in the field of Zoan;
44 and turned their rivers into blood, and their streams, so that they could not drink;
45 he sent dog-flies 3 among them which devoured them, and frogs, which destroyed them;
46 and he gave their increase to the caterpillar 4, and their labour to the locust;
47 he killed their vines with hail, and their sycamore trees with hail-stones;
48 and he delivered up their cattle to the hail, and their flocks to the thunderbolts.
49 He cast upon them the fierceness of his anger, wrath and indignation, and distress - a mission of angels of woes.
50 He made a way for his anger; he didn't spare their soul from death but gave their life over to the pestilence;
51 and he smote all the firstborn in Egypt, the firstfruits of their vigour in the tents of Ham.
52 And he made his own people go forth like sheep and guided them in the wilderness like a flock;
53 and he led them safely so that they were without fear; and the sea covered their enemies.
54 And he brought them to his holy border, this mountain, which his right hand purchased;
55 and he drove out the nations before them, and allotted them for an inheritance by line, and made the tribes of Israel to dwell in their tents.
56 But they tempted and provoked God, the Most High, and didn't keep his testimonies,
57 and they drew back and dealt treacherously like their fathers: they turned like a deceitful bow.

2 or 'limited'   3 or 'vermin' as in Exodus 8 v21
4 Literally 'the devourer', a species of locust

58 And they provoked him to anger with their high places, and moved him to jealousy with their graven images.
59 God heard and was wroth, and greatly abhorred Israel:
60 and he forsook the tabernacle at Shiloh, the tent where he had dwelt among men,
61 and gave his strength into captivity, and his glory 5 into the hand of the oppressor;
62 and delivered up his people to the sword, and was very wroth with his inheritance:
63 the fire consumed their young 6 men, and their maidens were not praised in [nuptial] song;
64 their priests fell by the sword and their widows made no lamentation 7.
65 Then the Lord awoke as one out of sleep, like a mighty man that shouts aloud by reason of wine;
66 and he smote his adversaries in the hinder part and put them to everlasting reproach.
67 And he rejected the tent of Joseph, and didn't choose the tribe of Ephraim,
68 but chose the tribe of Judah, the mount Zion which he loved;
69 and he built his sanctuary like the heights, like the earth which he has founded for ever.
70 And he chose David his servant, and took him from the sheepfolds:
71 from following the suckling-ewes, he brought him to feed Jacob his people, and Israel his inheritance.
72 And he fed them according to the integrity of his heart, and led them by the skilfulness of his hands.

---

5 Literally 'beauty'   6 or 'chosen' as in verse 31   7 or 'didn't weep'

Psalm 79
A psalm of Asaph

1 O God, the nations have come into your inheritance: they have defiled your holy temple; they have laid Jerusalem in heaps.
2 They have given the dead bodies of your servants to be meat to the fowl of the heavens, the flesh of your saints to the beasts of the earth:
3 they have shed their blood like water round about Jerusalem, and there was none to bury [them].
4 We have become a reproach to our neighbours, a mockery and a derision to them that are round about us.
5 How long, o Jehovah? Will you be angry for ever? Shall your jealousy burn like fire?
6 Pour out your fury upon the nations that have not known you, and upon the kingdoms that don't call upon your name:
7 for they have devoured Jacob and laid waste his habitation.
8 Don't remember against us the iniquities of [our] forefathers; let your tender mercies speedily come to meet us: for we are brought very low.
9 Help us, o God of our salvation, because of the glory of your name; and deliver us, and forgive our sins, for your name's sake.
10 Why should the nations say, "Where is their God?" Let the avenging of the blood of your servants that is shed be known among the nations in our sight.
11 Let the groaning of the prisoner come before you: according to the greatness of your arm preserve those that are appointed to die*:
12 and render to our neighbours sevenfold into their bosom, their reproach, wherewith they have reproached you, o Lord.
13 And we, your people and the sheep of your pasture, will give thanks to you for ever; we will show forth your praise from generation to generation.

* Literally 'the sons of death'

Psalm 80

To the chief Musician. On Shoshannim-Eduth. Of Asaph. A psalm.

1 Give ear, o Shepherd of Israel, you who leads Joseph like a flock; you who sits [between] the Cherubim*, shine forth.
2 Before Ephraim and Benjamin and Manasseh, stir up your strength and come to our deliverance.
3 O God, restore us; and cause your face to shine, and we shall be saved.
4 Jehovah, God of hosts, how long will your anger~ smoke against the prayer of your people?
5 You have fed them with the bread of tears and given them tears to drink in large measure:
6 you have made us a strife to our neighbours, and our enemies mock among themselves.
7 Restore us, o God of hosts; and cause your face to shine, and we shall be saved.
8 You brought a vine out of Egypt; you cast out the nations and planted it:
9 you prepared space before it and it took deep root and filled the land;
10 the mountains were covered with its shadow, and its branches were [like] the cedars of God^;
11 it sent out its boughs to the sea and its shoots to the river.
12 Why have you broken down its fences+ so that all who pass by the way do pluck it?
13 The boar out of the forest wastes it, and the beast^^ of the field feeds off it.
14 O God of hosts, return, we beseech you; look down from the heavens and behold, and visit this vine;
15 even the stock which** your right hand has planted, and the young plant~~ you made strong for yourself.
16 It is burned with fire, it is cut down; they perish at the rebuke of your countenance.
17 Let your hand be upon the man of your right hand, upon the son of man++ whom you have made strong for yourself.
18 So we will not go back from you. Revive us, and we will call upon your name.
19 Restore us, o Jehovah, God of hosts; cause your face to shine, and we shall be saved.

---

* or 'dwells above the cherubim', as in Psalm 99 v1   ~ Literally 'will you'
^ or 'great cedars' – see Psalm 36 6   + or 'enclosure-walls'
^^ or 'roaming creatures' as in Psalm 50 v11   ** others translate 'and protect that which'   ~~ Literally 'the son'   ++ or 'Adam's son' as Psalm 8 v4

Psalm 81

To the chief Musician. Upon the gittith. [A psalm] of Asaph

1 Sing joyously to God our strength, shout aloud to the God of Jacob;
2 raise a song, and sound the tambour, the pleasant harp with the lute.
3 Blow the trumpet at the new moon, at the set time*, on our feast day:
4 for this is a statute for Israel, an ordinance of the God of Jacob;
5 he ordained it in Joseph [for] a testimony, when he went forth over the land of Egypt, [where] I heard a language that I didn't know.
6 "I removed his shoulder from the burden; his hands were freed from the basket.
7 "You called in trouble and I delivered you; I answered you in the secret place of thunder; I proved you at the waters of Meribah. Selah.
8 "Hear, my people, and I will testify to you; o Israel, if you would hearken to me!
9 "There shall be no strange god in you, neither shall you worship any foreign god.
10 "I am Jehovah your God, that brought you up out of the land of Egypt: open your mouth wide and I will fill it.
11 "But my people didn't hearken to my voice and Israel would [have] none of me.
12 "So I gave them up to their own hearts' stubbornness: they walked after their own counsels.
13 "Oh that my people had hearkened to me, that Israel had walked in my ways!
14 "I would soon have subdued their enemies and turned my hand against their adversaries.
15 "The haters of Jehovah would have come cringing to him; but their time would have been for ever.
16 "And he would have fed them with the finest of wheat*; yes, with honey out of the rock I would have satisfied you."

* Literally 'the fat of wheat' – see Psalm 147 v14

Psalm 82
A psalm of Asaph

1 God stands in the assembly of God, he judges among the gods*.
2 "How long will you judge unrighteously, and accept the person of the wicked?" Selah.
3 "Judge~ the poor and the fatherless, do justice to the afflicted and the destitute;
4 "rescue the poor and needy, deliver them out of the hand of the wicked".
5 They don't know, neither do they understand; they walk on in darkness: all the foundations of the earth *(erets)* are moved.
6 I have said, "You are gods, and all of you are children of the Most High;
7 "but you shall die like men *(Adam)*, and fall like one of the princes".
8 Arise, o God, judge the earth *(erets)*; for you shall inherit all the nations.

* *elohim* 'the judges' See Exodus 21 v6
~ frequently means 'judge in favour of'

Psalm 83
A song: a psalm of Asaph.

1 O God, don't keep silence; don't hold your peace, and don't be still, o God:
2 for behold, your enemies make a tumult; and they that hate you lift up the head.
3 They take crafty counsel against your people, and consult against your hidden ones*:
4 they say, "Come, and let us cast them off from being a nation, and let the name of Israel be mentioned no more".
5 For they have consulted together with one heart: they have made an alliance together against you.
6 The tents of Edom and the Ishmaelites, Moab and the Hagarites;
7 Gebal and Ammon and Amalek; Philistia, with the inhabitants of Tyre;
8 Asshur~ is joined with them: they are an arm to the sons of Lot. Selah.
9 Do to them as to Midian; as to Sisera, as to Jabin, at the torrent of Kishon:
10 who were destroyed at Endor; they became as dung for the ground.
11 Make their nobles as Oreb and as Zeeb; and all their chiefs^ as Zebah and Zalmunna.
12 For they have said, "Let us take to ourselves God's dwelling-places in possession".
13 O my God, make them like a whirling thing, like stubble before the wind.
14 As fire burns a forest, and as the flame sets the mountains on fire,
15 so pursue them with your tempest and terrify them with your whirlwind.
16 Fill their faces with shame, that they may seek your name, o Jehovah.
17 Let them be put to shame and be dismayed for ever, and let them be confounded and perish:
18 that they may know that you alone, whose name is Jehovah+, are the Most High^^ over all the earth.

---

* see Psalm 31 v20   ~ Assyria   ^ Literally 'anointed ones' – see Ezekiel 32 v30
\+ or 'who alone has the name Jehovah'   ^^ Hebrew is *Elohim*

Psalm 84

To the chief Musician. Upon the gittith. Of the sons of Korah. A psalm.

1 How amiable are your tabernacles, o Jehovah of hosts!
2 My soul longs, yes, even faints for the courts of Jehovah; my heart and my flesh cry out for the living God.
3 Yes, the sparrow has found a house, and the swallow a nest for herself, where she lays her young, your altars, o Jehovah of hosts, my king and my God.
4 Blessed are they that dwell in your house: they will be constantly praising you. Selah.
5 Blessed is the man whose strength is in you – they in whose heart are the highways.
6 Passing through the valley of Baca* they make it a wellspring; yes, the early rain~ covers it with blessings.
7 They go from strength to strength: [each one] will appear before God in Zion.
8 Jehovah, God of hosts, hear my prayer; give ear, o God of Jacob. Selah.
9 Behold, o God our shield, and look upon the face of your anointed.
10 For a day in your courts is better than a thousand. I would rather stand at the threshold of the house of my God than dwell in the tents of wickedness.
11 For Jehovah-Elohim is a sun and shield: Jehovah will give grace and glory; no good thing will he withhold from them that walk uprightly.
12 Jehovah of hosts, blessed is the man that confides in you!

* or 'of weeping'
~ see Deuteronomy 11 v14 The autumn rain: the first with reference to the time of sowing

Psalm 85
To the chief Musician. Of the sons of Korah. A psalm.

1 You have been favourable. Jehovah, to your land; your have turned the captivity of Jacob:
2 you have forgiven the iniquity of your people: you have covered all their sin. Selah.
3 You have withdrawn all your wrath; you have turned from the fierceness of your anger.
4 Bring us back, o God of our salvation, and cause your indignation towards us to cease.
5 Will you be angry with us for ever? Will you draw out your anger from generation to generation?
6 Won't you revive us again that your people may rejoice in you?
7 Show us your loving-kindness, o Jehovah, and grant us your salvation.
8 I will hear what God, Jehovah, will speak; for he will speak peace to his people and to his godly ones *(chasid)*; but may they not return again to folly.
9 Surely his salvation is near them that fear him, that glory may dwell in our land.
10 Loving-kindness and truth are met together; righteousness and peace have kissed each other:
11 truth shall spring out of the earth, and righteousness shall look down from the heavens.
12 Jehovah also will give what is good, and our land shall yield its increase.
13 righteousness shall go before him, and shall set his footsteps on the way*.

* or 'shall set [itself] in the way of his steps'

Psalm 86
A prayer of David

1 Incline your ear, Jehovah, answer me; for I am afflicted and needy.
2 Keep my soul for I am godly*; you, o my God, save your servant who confides in you.
3 Be gracious to me, o Lord; for to you I call all the day.
4 Rejoice the soul of your servant; for to you, Lord, do I lift up my soul.
5 For you, Lord, are good, and ready to forgive~, and have great loving-kindness to all that call upon you.
6 Give ear, o Jehovah, to my prayer, and attend to the voice of my supplications.
7 In the day of my distress I will call upon you, for you will answer me.
8 Among the gods there is none like you, Lord, and there is nothing alike your works.
9 All nations whom you have made shall come and worship before you, o Lord, and shall glorify your name.
10 For you are great and do wondrous things: you are God, you alone.
11 Teach me your way, Jehovah; I will walk in your truth: unite my heart to fear your name.
12 I will praise^ you, o Lord my God, with my whole heart; and I will glorify your name for evermore.
13 For great is your loving-kindness toward me, and you have delivered my soul from the lowest Sheol.
14 O God, the proud are risen against me, and the assembly of the violent seek after my soul, and they have not set you before them.
15 But you, Lord, are a merciful and gracious God, slow to anger and abundant in goodness+ and truth.
16 Turn toward me and be gracious to me; give your strength to your servant and save the son of your handmaid.
17 Show me a token for good that they which hate me may see it and be ashamed; for you, Jehovah, have helped me and comforted me.

---

* or 'pious' 'holy' *(chasid)* – *chesed* is used for one who is the object of God's loving-kindness

~ Literally 'forgiving'   ^ or 'thank', same as Psalm 88 v10

+ or 'loving-kindness' *(chesed*

Psalm 87
Of the sons of Korah. A psalm. A song.

1 His foundation* is in the mountains of holiness.
2 Jehovah loves the gates of Zion more than all the habitations~ of jacob.
3 Glorious things are spoken of you, o city of God. Selah.
4 I will make mention of Rahab^ and Babylon among them that know me; behold Philistia and Tyre, with Ethiopia: this [man] was born there.
5 And of Zion it shall be said, "This one and that one was born in her"; and the Most High shall establish her.
6 Jehovah will count, when he inscribes the peoples, "This [man] was born there". Selah.
7 As well the singers as the dancers+ [shall say], "All my springs are in you".

* or 'What he has founded'   ~ or 'tabernacles'
^ that is, Egypt   + or 'pipers' 'players on instruments'

Psalm 88

A song, a psalm for the sons of Korah. To the chief Musician.
Upon mahalath-leannoth. An instruction. Of Heman the Ezrahite.

1 Jehovah, God of my salvation, I have cried by day [and] in the night before you.
2 Let my prayer come before you; incline your ear to my cry.
3 For my soul is full of troubles, and my life draws near to Sheol.
4 I am reckoned with them that go down into the pit; I am as a man that has no strength:
5 prostrate* among the dead, like the slain that lie in the grave; whom you remember no more, and who are cut off from your hand.
6 You have laid me in the lowest pit, in dark places~, in the deeps.
7 Your fury lies hard on me, and you have afflicted [me] with all your waves^. Selah.
8 You have put my familiar friends far from me; you have made me an abomination to them: I am shut up, and I cannot come forth.
9 Mine eye is consumed by reason of affliction. Upon you, Jehovah, I have called every day; I have stretched out my hands to you.
10 Will you do wonders+ to the dead? Shall the shades^^ arise and praise you?
11 Shall your loving-kindness be declared in the grave, your faithfulness in Destruction**?
12 Shall your wonders+ be known in the dark, and your righteousness in the land of forgetfulness?
13 But as for me, Jehovah, I cry to you, and in the morning my prayer comes before you~~.
14 Why, o Jehovah, do you cast off my soul? [Why] do you hide your face from me?
15 I am afflicted and expiring from my youth up; I suffer your terrors [and] I am distracted.
16 Your fierce anger++ has gone over me; your terrors have brought me to nought:
17 they have surrounded me all the day like water; they have encompassed me about together.
18 Lover and associate you have put far from me: my familiar friends are darkness.

---

* or 'cast away'   ~ or 'in darkness'. Literally 'darknesses'
^ strictly 'breakers' as in Psalm 42 v7   + Literally 'wonder'
^^ or 'the dead', 'those who are relaxed – feeble' as in Job 26 v5.
** Hebrew is *Abaddon*~~ Literally 'comes to meet you'
++ the Hebrew word is plural

Psalm 89
An instruction. Of Ethan the Ezrahite.

1 I will sing of the loving-kindness* of Jehovah for ever; with my mouth I will make known your faithfulness from generation to generation.
2 For I said, "Loving-kindness* shall be built up for ever"; in the very heavens you will establish your faithfulness.
3 I have made a covenant with my elect, I have sworn to David my servant:
4 "Your seed I will establish for ever, and build up your throne from generation to generation". Selah.
5 And the heavens shall celebrate~ your wonders^, o Jehovah, and your faithfulness in the congregation+ of the saints^^.
6 For who in the heaven** can be compared to Jehovah? [Who] among the sons of the mighty~~ shall be likened to Jehovah?
7 God is greatly to be feared in the council of the saints^^, and terrible for all that are round about him.
8 Jehovah, God of hosts, who is like you, the strong Jah? And your faithfulness is round about you.
9 You rule the pride of the sea: when its waves arise, you still them.
10 You have crushed Rahab++ as one that is slain; you have scattered your enemies with the arm of your strength.
11 Yours are the heavens, the earth also is yours; the world and its fulness, you have founded them.
12 The north and the south, you have created them: Tabor and Hermon triumph in your name.
13 Yours is the arm of might: strong is your hand, high is your right hand.
14 Righteousness and judgment are the foundation of your throne; loving-kindness and truth go before your face.
15 Blessed is the people that know the shout of joy: they walk, o Jehovah, in the light of your countenance.
16 In your name they are joyful all the day, and in your righteousness they are exalted.
17 For you are the glory of their strength; and in your favour our horn shall be exalted.

* Literally 'loving-kindnesses' 'mercies' *(chesed)* as in v 49. In verses 2,14,24,28,33 it's in the singular

~ elsewhere 'praise' 'confess'   ^ Literally 'wonders'   + As in Exodus 12 v6
^^ *kodesh* as in v18 'Holy One'; v20 'holy [oil]', 'holiness' in v35   ** or 'in the sky'
~~ or 'above'   ++ Egypt

18 For Jehovah is our shield and the Holy^^ One of Israel our king.
19 Then you spoke in visions of your Holy One *(chasid)*, and said, "I have laid help upon a mighty one; I have exalted one chosen 1 out of the people.
20 "I have found David my servant; with my holy^^ oil I have anointed him:
21 "with whom my hand shall be established; and my arm shall strengthen him.
22 "No enemy shall exact upon him, nor the son of wickedness afflict him;
23 "but I will beat down his adversaries before his face, and will smite them that hate him.
24 "And my faithfulness and my loving-kindness shall be with him, and by my name his horn shall be exalted.
25 "And I will set his hand in the sea and his right hand in the rivers.
26 "He shall call to me, "You are my father, my God, and the rock of my salvation;
27 "and as to me, I will make him firstborn, the highest 2 of the kings of the earth.
28 "My loving-kindness I will keep for him for evermore, and my covenant shall stand fast with him;
30 "If his sons forsake my law, and don't walk in my ordinances;
31 "if they profane my statutes and don't keep my commandments:
32 "then I will visit their transgressions with the rod, and their iniquity with stripes 3.
33 "Nevertheless my loving-kindness I won't utterly take from him nor belie my faithfulness;
34 "I won't profane my covenant, nor alter the thing that is gone out of my lips.
35 "Once I have sworn by my holiness^^; I will not lie to David:
36 "His seed shall endure for ever, and his throne as the sun before me;
37 "it shall be established for ever as the moon, and the witness in the sky is firm 4." Selah.
38 But you have rejected and cast off; you have been very wroth with your anointed:
39 you have made void the covenant of your servant; you have profaned his crown 5 to the ground:
40 you have broken down all his hedges; you have brought his strongholds to ruin.

1 or 'young man'
2 *elyon* see Psalm 83 v18   3 or 'plagues'   4 or 'steadfast'   5 elsewhere 'diadem'

41 All that pass by the way plunder him; he has become a reproach to his neighbours.
42 You have exalted the right hand of his oppressors; you have made all his enemies rejoice:
43 yes, you have turned back the edge of his sword and have not made him stand in the battle.
44 You have made his brightness cease and cast his throne down to the ground;
45 the days of his youth you have shortened; you have covered him with shame. Selah.
46 How long, Jehovah, will you hide yourself for ever? Shall your fury burn like fire?
47 Remember, as regards me, what life is. Why have created all the children of men to be vanity?
48 What man lives and shall not see death? Shall he deliver his soul from the power 6 of Sheol? Selah.
49 Where, Lord, are your former loving-kindnesses [which] you swore to David in your faithfulness?
50 Remember, Lord, the reproach of your servants – that I bear in my bosom [that of] all the mighty 7 peoples -
51 wherewith your enemies, o Jehovah, have reproached, wherewith they have reproached the footsteps of your anointed.

‡   ‡   ‡

52 Blessed be Jehovah for evermore! Amen, and Amen.

6 Literally 'hand'   7 Literally 'many' (i.e numerous)

FOURTH BOOK

Psalm 90
A prayer of Moses, the man of God

1 Lord, you have been our dwelling-place in all generations.
2 Before the mountains were brought forth* and you had formed~ the earth and the world *(tebel)*, even from eternity to eternity you are God.
3 You make [mortal] man return to dust^, and say, "Return, children of men".
4 For a thousand years in your sight are as yesterday when it is past, and [as] a watch in the night.
5 You carry them away as with a flood; they are [as] a sleep: in the morning they are like grass [that] grows up:
6 in the morning it flourishes and grows up; in the evening it is cut down and withers.
7 For we are consumed by your anger, and by your fury we are troubled.
8 You have set our iniquities before you, our secret [sins] in the light of your countenance.
9 For all our days pass away in your wrath: we spend our years as a [passing] thought.
10 The days of our years are threescore years and ten; and if by reason of strength they are fourscore years, their pride is labour and vanity+, for it is soon cut off and we fly away.
11 Who knows the power of your anger, and your wrath according to the fear of you?
12 So teach [us] to number our days that we may acquire a wise heart.
13 Return, Jehovah: how long? And let it repent you^^ concerning your servants.
14 Satisfy us early** with your loving-kindness; that we may sing for joy and be glad all our days.
15 Make us glad according to the days [in which] you have afflicted us, according to the years [in which] we have seen evil.
16 Let your work appear to your servants, and your majesty to~~ their sons.
17 And let the beauty++ of Jehovah our God be upon us; and establish the work of our hands upon us; yes, the work of our hands, establish it.

---

* or 'given birth to'   ~ or 'brought forth'   ^ Literally 'to crumbling'
+ these words are rendered 'mischief and iniquity' when presented actively
^^ or 'be merciful to'   ** or 'in the morning'   ~~ or 'upon'
++ or 'pleasantness' as in Psalm 27

Psalm 91

1 He that dwells in the secret place of the Most High* shall abide under the shadow of the Almighty~.
2 I say of Jehovah, "My refuge and my fortress; my God, I will confide in him".
3 Surely^ he shall deliver you from the snare of the fowler, [and] from the destructive pestilence.
4 He shall cover you with his feathers, and under his wings you shall find refuge: his truth is a shield and buckler.
5 You shall not be afraid for the terror by night, for the arrow that flies by day,
6 for the pestilence that walks in darkness, for the destruction that wastes at noonday.
7 A thousand shall fall at your side, and ten thousand at your right hand [but] it shall not come near you.
8 Only with your eyes you shall behold, and see the reward of the wicked.
9 Because you have made Jehovah, my refuge, the Most High, your dwelling-place,
10 no evil shall befall you, neither shall any plague come near your tent.
11 For he shall give his angels charge concerning you to keep you in all your ways:
12 they shall bear you up in [their] hands in case you dash your foot+ against a stone.
13 You shall tread upon the lion^^ and the adder; the young lion and the dragon** you shall trample under foot.
14 Because he has set his love upon me, therefore I will deliver him; I will set him on high~~ because he has known my name.
15 He shall call upon me and I will answer him; I will be with him in trouble, I will deliver him and honour him.
16 With length of days I will satisfy him, and show him my salvation.

---

* *Elyon* as in Psalm 83 v18   ~ *Shaddai* as in Genesis 17 v1 and Exodus 6 v3
^ or 'For'   + or 'in case your foot stumbles'   ^^ strictly 'a fierce lion'
** or 'sea monster' or 'serpent' – the same word is used for sea and rivers, could include crocodiles, serpents etc
~~ see Psalm 20 v1 and Psalm 69 v29

Psalm 92
A psalm, a song, for the sabbath day

1 It is good to give thanks to Jehovah, and to sing psalms to your name, o Most High:
2 to declare your loving-kindness in the morning and your faithfulness in the nights.
3 Upon an instrument of ten strings and upon the lute; upon the higgaion with the harp.
4 For you, Jehovah, have made me glad through your work*; I will triumph in the works of your hands.
5 Jehovah, how great are your works! Your thoughts are very deep:
6 a brutish~ man does not know, neither does a fool *(kesil)* understand it.
7 When the wicked spring as the grass, and when all the workers of iniquity flourish, it is that that may be destroyed for ever.
8 And you, Jehovah, are on high for evermore.
9 For lo, your enemies, o Jehovah, for lo, your enemies shall perish; all the workers of iniquity shall be scattered.
10 But my horn you shall exalt like a buffalo's: I shall be anointed^ with fresh oil.
11 And my eyes shall see [its desire] on my enemies; my ears shall hear [it] of the evildoers that rise up against me.
12 The righteous shall shoot forth like a palm-tree; he shall grow like a cedar on Lebanon.
13 Those that are planted in the house of Jehovah shall flourish in the courts of our God:
14 they are still vigorous+ in old age, they are full of sap and green;
15 to show that Jehovah is upright: [he is] my rock, and there is no unrighteousness in him.

---

* *poal* as Isaiah 45 v9 – 'finished work' done with a purpose; 'works' in verse 5 is *masseh* as in 'occupation'   ~ see Psalm 49 v10
^ strictly 'mingled' per Leviticus 2 v4: mingled indicates more than anointed: the whole system is invigorated and strengthened by it
+ or 'shall still bear fruit' as 'increase like in Psalm 62 v10

Psalm 93

1 Jehovah reigns, he has clothed himself with majesty: Jehovah has clothed himself , he has girded himself with strength; yes, the world is established, it shall not be moved.
2 Your throne is established of old; you are from eternity.
3 The floods* lifted up, o Jehovah, the floods* lifted up their voice; the floods* lifted up their roaring waves.
4 Jehovah on high is mightier than the voices of many waters, than the mighty breakers of the sea.
5 Your testimonies are very sure: holiness is becoming to your house, o Jehovah, for ever~.

* or 'rivers' - see Psalm 98 v8   ~ or 'length of days'

Psalm 94

1 God of vengeances, Jehovah, God of vengeances, shine forth;
2 lift up yourself, judge of the earth, render the reward to the proud.
3 How long shall the wicked, o Jehovah, how long shall the wicked triumph?
4 [How long] shall they utter [and] speak insolence – all the workers of iniquity boast themselves?
5 They crush your people, o Jehovah, and afflict your inheritance;
6 they slay the widow and the stranger and murder the fatherless,
7 and say, "Jah will not see, neither will the God of Jacob regard [it]".
8 Understand, you brutish among the people; and you fools, when will you be wise?
9 He that planted the ear, shall he not hear? He that formed the eye, shall he not see?
10 He that instructs* the nations, shall he not correct – he that teaches man knowledge?
11 Jehovah knows the thoughts of man, that they are vanity~.
12 Blessed is the man *(geber)* whom you chasten, o Jah, and whom you teach out of your law;
13 that you may give him rest from the days of evil, until the pit be digged for the wicked.
14 For Jehovah will not cast off his people neither will he forsake his inheritance;
15 for judgment shall return to righteousness, and all the upright in heart shall follow it^.
16 Who will rise up for me against the evildoers? Who will stand for me against the workers of iniquity?
17 If Jehovah had not been my help, my soul had almost+ dwelt in silence.
18 When I said, "My foot is slipping", your loving-kindness, o Jehovah, held me up.
19 In the multitude of my anxious thoughts within me your comforts have delighted my soul.
20 Shall the throne of wickedness^^ be united to you, which frames mischief into a law?
21 They band together against the soul of the righteous and condemn innocent blood.

* or 'chastens'   ~ or 'a breath' – see Psalm 39 v5,6,11 etc
^ that is, judgment   + or 'soon'
^^ see Psalm 55 v11 'perversities' and note for Psalm 5 v9

22 But Jehovah will be my high tower; and my God the rock of my refuge.
23 And he will bring upon them their iniquity, and will cut them off in their own evil: Jehovah our God will cut them off.

Psalm 95

1 Come, let us sing aloud to Jehovah, let us shout for joy to the rock of our salvation;
2 let us come before him with thanksgiving; let us shout aloud to him with psalms.
3 For Jehovah is a great God, and a great king above all gods.
4 In his hand are the deep places of the earth; the heights* of the mountains are his also:
5 the sea is his, and he made it, and his hands formed the dry [land].
6 Come, let us worship and kneel before Jehovah our Maker.
7 For he is our God; and we are the people of his pasture and the sheep of his hand. Today if you hear his voice,
8 do not harden your heart as at Meribah~, as [in] the day of Massah^ in the wilderness;
9 when your fathers tempted me, proved me, and saw my work.
10 Forty years I was grieved+ with the generation and said, "It is a people that errs in their heart, and they have not known my ways";
11 so that I swore^^ in my anger that they should not enter into my rest.

---

* or 'treasures' as in Job 22 v25 'heaped up'   ~ 'strife'   ^ 'temptation'
\+ the word implies loathing   ^^ or 'unto whom I swore'

Psalm 96*

1 Sing to Jehovah a new song: sing to Jehovah, all the earth.
2 Sing to Jehovah, bless his name; publish his salvation from day to day.
3 Declare his glory among the nations, his wondrous works among all the peoples.
4 For Jehovah is great and exceedingly to be praised; he is terrible above all gods.
5 For all the gods of the people are idols~; but Jehovah made the heavens.
6 Majesty and splendour are before him; strength and beauty are in his sanctuary.
7 Give to Jehovah, you families of people, give to Jehovah glory and strength;
8 give to Jehovah the glory of his name; bring an oblation and come into his courts;
9 worship Jehovah in holy splendour; tremble before him, all the earth.
10 Say among the nations, "Jehovah reigns!" Yes, the world *(tebel)* is established, it shall not be moved; he will execute judgment upon the peoples with equity.
11 Let the heavens rejoice, and let the earth be glad; let the sea roar, and all its fulness;
12 let the field exult and all that is therein. Then all the trees of the forest shall sing for joy,
13 before Jehovah, for he comes; for he comes to judge the earth: he will judge the world *(tebel)* with righteousness, and the peoples in his faithfulness.

* See 1 Chronicles 16 v23-33 from which most of this psalm derives
~ or 'nonentities' – see Psalm 97 v7

Psalm 97

1 Jehovah reigns: let the earth be glad, let the many isles rejoice.
2 Clouds and darkness are round about him; righteousness and judgment are the foundation of his throne.
3 A fire goes before him, and burns up his adversaries round about.
4 His lightnings lightened the world: the earth saw and trembled.
5 The mountains melted like wax at the presence of Jehovah, at the presence of the Lord of the whole earth.
6 The heavens declare his righteousness and all the peoples see* his glory.
7 All those who serve graven images be ashamed, that boast themselves of idols. Worship him, all you gods~.
8 Zion heard, and rejoiced; and the daughters of Judah were glad because of your judgments, o Jehovah.
9 For you, Jehovah, are the Most High above all the earth; you are exalted exceedingly above all gods.
10 You that love Jehovah, hate evil: he preserves the souls of his saints^, he delivers them out of the hand of the wicked.
11 Light is sown for the righteous+, and joy for the upright in heart.
12 Rejoice in Jehovah, you righteous; and give thanks in remembrance^^ of his holiness.

* or 'declared.....saw'   ~ or 'angels' *elohim*   ^ or 'godly ones' *(chasid)* see note for Psalm 86 v2   + Hebrew word is singular
^^ see Exodus 3 v15 and 'holiness' in this verse is *kodesh*

Psalm 98

1 Sing to Jehovah a new song: for he has done wondrous things; his right hand and his holy arm have wrought salvation for him.
2 Jehovah has made known his salvation: he has openly showed his righteousness in the sight of the nations.
3 He has remembered his loving-kindness and his faithfulness toward the house of Israel: all the ends of the earth have seen the salvation of our God.
4 Shout aloud to Jehovah, all the earth; break forth and shout for joy, and sing psalms.
5 Sing psalms to Jehovah with the harp: with the harp and the voice of a song;
6 with trumpets and sound of cornet, make a joyful noise* before the king, Jehovah.
7 Let the sea roar, and its fulness; the world, and they that dwell therein;
8 let the floods clap [their] hands; let the mountains sing for joy together,
9 before Jehovah, for he comes to judge the world with righteousness and the peoples with equity.

* or 'shout aloud' as verse 4

Psalm 99

1 Jehovah reigns: let the peoples tremble. He sits [between the] cherubim*: let the earth be moved.
2 Jehovah is great in Zion, and he is high above all the peoples.
3 They shall praise~ your great and terrible name – it is holy^ -
4 and the strength of the king that loves justice. You have established equity: it is you that executes judgment and righteousness in Jacob.
5 Exalt Jehovah our God, and worship at his footstool. He is holy!^
6 Moses and Aaron among his priests, and Samuel among them that call on his name: they called to Jehovah and he answered them.
7 He spoke to them in the pillar of cloud: they kept his testimonies and the statute that he gave them.
8 Jehovah, our God, you answered them: you were a forgiving God to them, though you took vengeance of their doings.
9 Exalt Jehovah our God, and worship at the hill of his holiness; for holy^ is Jehovah our God.

* see note Psalm 80 v1 or 'dwells above the cherubim'   ~ or 'thank'
^ *kadosh* see Psalm 16 v3

Psalm 100
A psalm of thanksgiving.

1 Shout aloud* to Jehovah, all the earth!
2 Serve Jehovah with joy: come before his presence with exultation.
3 Know that Jehovah is God: it is he that has made us and not we ourselves~; [we are] his people, and the sheep of his pasture.
4 Enter into his gates with thanksgiving [and] into his courts with praise; give thanks to him, bless his name:
5 for Jehovah is good; his loving-kindness [endures] for ever; and his faithfulness from generation to generation.

* or 'make a joyful noise' like Psalm 98 v4,6 – 'earth' might be read as 'land'
~ others 'and we are his'

Psalm 101
A psalm of David.

1 I will sing of loving-kindness and judgment: to you, Jehovah, I will sing psalms.
2 I will behave myself wisely in a perfect way. When will you come to me? I will walk within my house in the integrity of my heart.
3 I will set no thing of Belial before my eyes: I hate the work of them that turn aside; it shall not cleave to me.
4 A perverse heart shall depart from me; I will not know evil*.
5 Whoever secretly slanders his neighbour, I will destroy him; he that has a high look and a proud heart I will not suffer.
6 My eyes shall be upon the faithful of the land, that they may dwell with me; he that walks in a perfect way, he shall serve me.
7 He that practises deceit shall not dwell within my house; he that speaks falsehood shall not subsist in my sight.
8 Every morning I will destroy all the wicked of the land: to cut off all the workers of iniquity from the city of Jehovah.

* or 'an evil person'

Psalm 102

A prayer of the afflicted, when he is overwhelmed
and pours out his complaint before Jehovah.

1 Jehovah, hear my prayer, and let my cry come to you.
2 Don't hide your face from me: in the day of my trouble, incline your ear to me; in the day I call, answer me speedily.
3 For my days are consumed like smoke, and my bones are burned as a firebrand.
4 My heart is smitten and withered like grass; yes*, I have forgotten to eat my bread.
5 By reason of the voice of my groaning, my bones cleave to my flesh.
6 I have become like a pelican of the wilderness, I am as an owl in desolate places;
7 I watch, and am like a sparrow alone upon the house-top.
8 My enemies reproach me all the day; they that are mad against me swear by me.
9 For I have eaten ashes like bread, and mingled my drink with weeping,
10 because of your indignation and your wrath~; for you have lifted me up, and cast me down.
11 My days are like a lengthened-out shadow, and I, I am withered like grass.
12 But you, Jehovah, abide for ever, and your memorial^ from generation to generation.
13 You will rise up, you will have mercy upon Zion: for it is the time to be gracious to her for the set time has come.
14 For your servants take pleasure in her stones and favour+ her dust.
15 And the nations shall fear the name of Jehovah, and all the kings of the earth your glory.
16 When Jehovah shall build up Zion, he will appear in his glory.
17 He will regard the prayer of the destitute one and not despise their prayer.
18 This shall be written for the generation to come; and a people that shall be created shall praise Jah:
19 for he has looked down from the height of his sanctuary; from the heavens Jehovah has beheld the earth,

---

* or 'for'   ~ see note for Psalm 38 v1,3
^ see Exodus 3 v15 – where God makes his name known, referencing Abraham, Isaac and Jacob   + or 'are gracious to' like in verse 13

20 to hear the groaning of the prisoner, to loose those that are appointed to die^^;
21 that the name of Jehovah may be declared in Zion, and his praise in Jerusalem,20 to hear the groaning of the prisoner, to loose those that are appointed to die^^;
21 that the name of Jehovah may be declared in Zion, and his praise in Jerusalem,
22 when the peoples shall be gathered together, and the kingdoms, to serve Jehovah.
23 He weakened my strength in the way, he shortened my days.
24 I said, "My God, don't take me away in the midst of my days! ...Your years are from generation to generation"**.
25 Of old you have founded the earth, and the heavens are the work of your hands:
26 they shall perish, but you continue; and all of them shall grow old as a garment: as a vesture you shall change them, and they shall be changed.
27 But you are the Same~~ and your years shall have no end.
28 The children of your servants shall abide++ and their seed shall be established before you.

^^ Literally 'the sons of death'
** Literally 'in generation of generations' see Psalm 72 5
~~ Literally 'You He' a name of God, 'The existing One, who does not change' see Deuteronomy 32 v39
++ or 'dwell' see Psalm 37 v27, 29

Psalm 103
[A psalm] of David

1 Bless Jehovah, o my soul; and all that is within me, [bless] his holy name!
2 Bless Jehovah, o my soul, and don't forget all his benefits:
3 who forgives all your iniquities, who heals all your diseases;
4 who redeems your life from the pit, who crowns you with loving-kindness and tender mercies;
5 who satisfies your old age* with good [things]; your youth is renewed like the eagle's.
6 Jehovah executes righteousness and justice~ for all that are oppressed.
7 He made known his ways to Moses, his acts^ to the children of Israel.
8 Jehovah is merciful and gracious, slow to anger, and abundant in loving-kindness.
9 He will not always chide, neither will he keep [his anger] for ever.
10 He has not dealt with us according to our sins, nor rewarded us according to our iniquities.
11 For as the heavens are high above the earth, so great is+ his loving-kindness toward them that fear him.
12 As far as the east is from the west, so far has he removed our transgressions from us.
13 As a father pities [his] children, so Jehovah pities them that fear him.
14 For he knows our frame; he remembers that we are dust.
15 As for man *(enosh),* his days are as grass; as a flower of the field, so he flourishes:
16 for the wind passes over it and it is gone, and the place thereof knows it no more.
17 But the loving-kindness of Jehovah is from everlasting and to everlasting, upon them that fear him and his righteousness to children's children,
18 to such as keep his covenant and to those that remember to do his precepts.
19 Jehovah has established his throne in the heavens and his kingdom rules over all.

* or 'adornment' or 'mouth'   Literally 'righteousnesses and judgments'
^ or 'doings' 'exploits' – see Psalms 66 v5, 78 v11, 105 v1
+ Literally 'so has prevailed'

20 Bless Jehovah, you his angels, mighty in strength, that execute his word, hearkening to the voice of his word.

21 Bless Jehovah, all you his hosts; you ministers of his that do his will^^.

22 Bless Jehovah, all his works, in all places of his dominion. Bless Jehovah, o my soul.

^^ or 'good pleasure' as Psalm 51 v18

Psalm 104

1 Bless Jehovah, o my soul! Jehovah my God, you are very great; you are clothed with majesty and splendour;
2 covering yourself with light as with a garment, stretching out the heavens like a curtain -
3 who lays the beams of his upper chambers in the waters, who makes clouds his chariot, who walks upon the wings of the wind;
4 who makes* his angels spirits, his ministers a flame of fire.
5 He laid the earth upon its foundations: it shall not be removed for ever.
6 You had covered it with the deep, as with a vesture; the waters stood above the mountains;
7 at your rebuke they fled, at the voice of your thunder they hasted away -
8 the mountains rose, the valleys sank, to the place which you had founded for them -
9 you set a boundary which they may not pass over, that they do not turn again to cover the earth.
10 He sends the springs into the valleys: they run among the mountains;
11 they give drink to every beast of the field; the wild asses quench their thirst.
12 The birds of heaven dwell by them; they give forth their voice from among the branches.
13 He waters the mountains from his upper-chambers: the earth is satisfied with the fruit of your works~.
14 He makes the grass grow for the cattle, and herb for the service of man; bringing forth bread out of the earth,
15 and wine which gladdens the heart of man *(enosh)*; making [his] face shine with oil; and with bread he strengthens man's *(enosh)* heart
16 The trees of Jehovah are satisfied, the cedars of Lebanon, which he has planted,
17 where the birds make their nests; [as for] the stork, the fir trees^ are her house.
18 The high mountains are for the wild goats; the cliffs a refuge for the rock-badgers+.
19 He made the moon for seasons: the suns knows its going down.

---

* i.e. he created them so   ~ *Masseh* as 'occupation' see Psalm 92 v4
^ or 'cypresses' as in 1 Kings 5 v10 etc   + as Leviticus 11 v5 Syrian hyrax

20 You make darkness, and it is night, when all the beasts of the forest creep forth:
21 the young lions roar after its prey, and to seek their food from God.
22 The sun rises, they retreat and lie down in their dens.
23 Man *(Adam)* goes forth to his work and to his labour until the evening.
24 How manifold are your works~, o Jehovah! In wisdom you have made them all: the earth is full of your riches.
25 Yonder is the great and wide sea: in it are innumerable moving things, living creatures small and great.
26 There go the ships; [there] that leviathan^^ which you have formed to play therein.
27 These all look to you that you may give their food in its season:
28 what you give to them, they gather; you open your hand, they are filled with good.
29 You hide your face, they are troubled; you take away their breath, they expire and return to the dust.
30 You send forth your spirit, they are created; and you renew the face of the earth.
31 The glory of Jehovah will endure for ever; Jehovah will rejoice in his works~.
32 He looks on the earth and it trembles; he touches the mountains and they smoke.
33 I will sing to Jehovah as long as I live; I will sing psalms to my God while I have my being.
34 My meditation shall be pleasant to him**; I will rejoice in Jehovah.
35 Sinners shall be consumed out of the earth and the wicked shall be no more. Bless Jehovah, o my soul. Hallelujah!

~ *masseh* as 'occupation' Genesis 6 v43; see also Psalm 92 v4
^^ probably a species of whale. The great sea is the Mediterranean
** or 'My meditation of him shall be pleasant'

Psalm 105

1 Give thanks to Jehovah, call upon his name; make known his acts among the peoples.
2 Sing to him, sing psalms to him; meditate upon* all his wondrous works.
3 Glory in his holy name: let the heart of them rejoice that seek Jehovah.
4 Seek Jehovah and his strength, seek his face continually;
5 remember his wondrous works which he has done, his miracles and the judgments~ of his mouth:
6 you seed of Abraham his servant, you sons of Jacob, his chosen ones.
7 He, Jehovah, is our God; his judgments are in all the earth.
8 He is ever mindful of his covenant – the word which he commanded to a thousand generations -
9 which he made with Abraham, and of his oath to Isaac;
10 and he confirmed it to Jacob for a statute, to Israel for an everlasting covenant,
11 saying, "To you I will give the land of Canaan, the lot of your inheritance";
12 when they were a few men^ in number, of small account and strangers in it.
13 And they went from nation to nation, from one kingdom to another people.
14 He suffered no man to oppress them, and reproved kings for their sakes,
15 [saying], "Do not touch my anointed ones, and do not harm my prophets".
16 And he called for a famine upon the land; he broke the whole staff of bread.
17 He sent a man before them: Joseph was sold for a bondman.
18 They afflicted his feet with fetters; his soul came into irons;
19 until the time when what he said *(dabar)* came about: the word *(imrah)* of Jehovah tried him.
20 The king sent and loosed him – the ruler of peoples – and let him go free.
21 He made him lord of his house, and ruler over all his possessions:
22 to bind his princes at his pleasure, and teach his elders wisdom.
23 And Israel came into Egypt, and Jacob sojourned in the land of

---

* or 'talk of'   ~ or 'ordinances'
^ see Deuteronomy 4 v27 i.e. that could be numbered

Ham.

24 And he made his people exceeding fruitful, and made them mightier than their oppressors.

25 He turned their heart to hate his people, to deal subtly with his servants.

26 He sent Moses his servant, [and] Aaron whom he had chosen:

27 they set his signs among them, and miracles in the land of Ham.

28 He sent darkness and made it dark; and they did not rebel against his word.

29 He turned their waters into blood, and caused their fish to die.

30 Their land swarmed with frogs – in the chambers of their kings.

31 He spoke, and there came dog-flies [and] gnats in all their borders.

32 He gave them hail for rain, [and] flaming fire in their land;

33 and he smote their vines and their fig-trees, and broke the trees of their borders.

34 He spoke, and the locust came and the cankerworm^^, even without number;

35 and they devoured every herb in their land, and ate up the fruit of their ground.

36 And he smote every firstborn in their land, the firstfruits of all their vigour.

37 And he brought them forth with silver and gold; and there was not one feeble** among their tribes.

38 Egypt rejoiced in their departure; for the fear of them had fallen upon them.

39 He spread a cloud for a covering, and fire to give light in the night.

40 They asked, and he brought quails, and satisfied them with the bread of heaven.

41 He opened the rock, and waters gushed forth; they ran in the dry places [like] a river.

42 For he remembered his holy word, [and] Abraham his servant;

43 and he brought forth his people with gladness, his chosen~~ with rejoicing++;

44 and he gave them the lands of the nations, and they took possession of the labour of the peoples *(leummim)*:

45 that they might keep his statutes and observe his laws. Hallelujah!

---

^ Literally 'the feeder', a species of locust, most likely as it is   developing and not yet perfect, where it devours voraciously   ** or 'that stumbled'   ~~ as 'elect'   ++ or 'songs of triumph'

Psalm 106

1 Hallelujah! Give thanks to Jehovah; for he* is good; for his loving-kindness [endures] for ever.
2 Who can utter the mighty acts of Jehovah? [Who] can show forth all his praise?
3 Blessed are they that keep justice [and] he that does righteouness at all times.
4 Remember me, o Jehovah, with [your] favour toward your people; visit me with your salvation:
5 that I may see the prosperity of your chosen ones, that I may rejoice in the joy of your nation, that I may glory with your inheritance.
6 We have sinned with our fathers, we have committed iniquity, we have done wickedly.
7 Our fathers in Egypt did not consider your wondrous works; they did not remember the multitude of your loving-kindnesses, but they rebelled~ at the sea, at the Red Sea.
8 Yet he saved them for his name's sake, that he might make known his might.
9 And he rebuked the Red Sea, and it dried up; and he led them through the deeps as through a wilderness^.
10 And he saved them from the hand of him that hated [them], and redeemed them from the hand of the enemy.
11 And the waters covered their oppressors: not one of them was left.
12 Then they believed his words; they sang his praise.
13 They soon forgot his works; they didn't wait for his counsel:
14 and they lusted exceedingly in the wilderness, and tempted God in the desert.
15 The he gave them their request but sent leanness into their soul.
16 And they envied Moses in the camp,[and] Aaron, the saint+ of Jehovah.
17 The earth opened and swallowed up Dathan, and covered the company of Abiram;
18 and fire was kindled in their company; a flame burned up the wicked.
19 They made a calf in Horeb, and did homage to a molten image;
20 and they changed their glory into the similitude of an ox that eats grass.

---

* or 'it' same in Psalm 107 v1   ~ or 'provoked [him]' as in verse 43
^ or 'the wilderness'   + or 'holy one' (*kodesh*) see Psalms 16 v3, 89 v18

21 They forgot God their Saviour who had done great things in Egypt,
22 wondrous works in the land of Ham, terrible things by the Red Sea.
23 And he said that he would destroy them had not Moses, his chosen, stood in the breach to turn away his fury in case he should destroy [them].
24 And they despised the pleasant land; they did not believe his word,
25 but murmured in their tents: they did not hearken to the voice of Jehovah.
26 And he lifted up his hand^^ to them, that he would make them fall in the wilderness;
27 and that he would make their seed fall among the nations, and disperse them through the countries.
28 And they joined themselves to Baal-Peor and ate the sacrifices of the dead;
29 and they provoked [him] to anger with their doings; and a plague broke out among them.
30 Then Phinehas stood up and executed judgment and the plague was stayed;
31 and that was reckoned to him for righteousness, from generation to generation, for evermore.
32 And they moved him to wrath at the waters of Meribah, and it went ill with Moses on their account;
33 for they provoked his spirit so that he spoke unadvisedly with his lips.
34 They did not destroy the peoples as** Jehovah commanded them;
35 but they mingled with the nations and learned their works;
36 and they served their idols, and they were a snare to them:
37 and they sacrificed their sons and their daughters to demons,
38 and shed innocent blood, the blood of their sons and of their daughters whom they sacrificed to the idols of Canaan; and the land was polluted with blood.
39 And they were defiled with their works, and went a-whoring~~ in their doings.
40 Then the anger of Jehovah was kindled against his people, and he abhorred his inheritance;
41 and he gave them into the hand of the nations; and they that hated them ruled over them:

---

^^ i.e. he swore – see Exodus 6 v8   ** or 'concerning whom'
~~ other translations 'they defiled themselves'

42 and their enemies oppressed them, and they were brought into subjection under their hand.
43 Often he delivered them; but as for them, they provoked [him] by their counsel and they were brought low by their iniquity.
44 But he regarded their distress when he heard their cry;
45 and he remembered for them his covenant, and repented according to the multitiude of his loving-kindnesses;
46 and he caused them to find compassion of all those that had carried them captives.
47 Save us, Jehovah our God, and gather us from among the nations, to give thanks to your holy name [and] to triumph in your praise.

‡ ‡ ‡

48 Blessed be Jehovah the God of Israel, from eternity and eternity! And let all the people say, "Amen!" Hallelujah!

FIFTH BOOK

Psalm 107

1 Give thanks to Jehovah; for he is good; for his loving-kindness [endures] for ever.
2 Let the redeemed of Jehovah say so, whom he has redeemed from the hand of the oppressor,
3 and gathered out of the countries, from the east and from the west, from the north and from the sea.
4 They wandered in the wilderness in a desert way, they found no city of habitation;
5 hungry and thirsty, their soul fainted in them:
6 then they cried to Jehovah in their trouble [and] he delivered them out of their distresses,
7 and he led them forth by a right way that they might go to a city of habitation.
8 Let them give thanks to Jehovah for his loving-kindness, and for his wondrous works to the children of men;
9 for he has satisfied the longing soul and filled the hungry soul with good.
10 Such as inhabit darkness and the shadow of death, bound in affliction and iron,
11 because they had rebelled against the words of God and had despised the counsel of the Most High...
12 and he bowed down their heart with labour; they stumbled, and there was none to help:
13 then they cried to Jehovah in their trouble, [and] he saved them out of their distresses;
14 he brought them out of darkness and the shadow of death and broke their bands in sunder.
15 Let them give thanks to Jehovah for his loving-kindness and his wondrous works to the children of men;
16 for he has broken the gates of bronze and cut asunder the bars of iron.
17 Fools, because of their way of transgression, and because of their iniquities, are afflicted;
18 their soul abhors all manner of food, and they draw near to the gates of death:
19 then they cry to Jehovah in their trouble, [and] he saves them out of their distresses;

20 he sends his word and heals them, and delivers them from their destructions*.
21 Let them give thanks to Jehovah for his loving-kindness and his wondrous works to the children of men,
22 and let them offer~ the sacrifices of thanksgiving^, and declare his works in joyful song+.
23 They that go down to the sea in ships, that do business in great waters,
24 these see the works of Jehovah and his wonders in the deep.
25 For he speaks, and raises the stormy wind, which lifts up the waves;
26 they mount up to the heavens, they go down to the depths; their soul is melted because of trouble;
27 they reel to and fro, and stagger like a drunken man, and they are at their wits' end:
28 then they cry to Jehovah in their trouble, and he brings them out of their distresses;
29 he makes the storm a calm, and the waves [of the sea] are still:
30 and they rejoice because they are quiet; and he brings them to their desired haven.
31 Let them give thanks to Jehovah for his loving-kindness and his wondrous works to the children of men;
32 let them exalt him also in the congregation of the people, and praise him in the session of the elders.
33 He makes rivers into a wilderness, and water-springs into dry ground;
34 a fruitful land into a plain of salt for the wickedness of them that dwell therein.
35 He makes the wilderness into a pool of water, and the dry land into water-springs;
36 and there he makes the hungry to dwell, and they establish a city of habitation;
37 and sow fields, and plant vineyards, which yield fruits of increase;
38 and he blesses them so that they are multiplied greatly; and he does not suffer their cattle to decrease.
39 And they are diminished and brought low, through oppression, adversity and sorrow:
40 he pours contempt upon nobles, and causes them to wander in a pathless waste;

---

* Literally 'pits' and so 'pit-falls'
~ *zavach* Literally 'sacrifice' as Psalms 4 v5, 27 v6, 50 v14, 23 etc
^ see Levitcus 7 v12   + or 'with rejoicing'

41 but he secures the needy one on high from affliction, and makes [him] families like flocks.
42 The upright shall see it and rejoice; and all unrighteousness shall stop its mouth.
43 Whoever is wise, let him observe these things, and let them^^ understand the loving-kindnesses *(chesed)* of Jehovah.

^^ or 'Whoever is wise, and observes these things, even [they] shall...'

Psalm 108*
A song, a psalm of David

1 My heart is fixed, o God: I will sing, yes, I will sing psalms, even [with] my glory.
2 Awake, lute and harp: I will wake the dawn.
3 I will give you thanks among the peoples *(ammim)*, o Jehovah; I will sing psalms of you among the nations *(leummim)*:
4 for your loving-kindness is great above the heavens and your truth is to the clouds.
5 Be exalted above the heavens, o God, and your glory above all the earth.
6 That your beloved ones may be delivered: save with your right hand, and answer me.
7 God has spoken in his holiness: I will exult, I will divide Shechem and mete out the valley of Succoth.
8 Gilead is mine, Manasseh is mine, and Ephraim is the strength~ of my head; Judah is my law-giver;
9 Moab is my wash-pot; upon Edom I will cast my sandal; over Philistia I will shout aloud.
10 Who will bring me into the strong city? Who will lead me to Edom?
11 [Will] you not, o God, who had cast us off and did not go forth, o God, with our armies?
12 Give us help from trouble; for vain is man's deliverance.
13 Through God we shall do valiantly; and he it is that will tread down our adversaries *(tzar)*.

* Compare this psalm with Psalm 57 v7-11 and Psalm 60 v5-12
~ or 'defence'

Psalm 109

To the chief Musician. Of David. A psalm

1 O God of my praise, do not be silent:
2 for the mouth of the wicked [man] and the mouth of deceit are opened against me: they have spoken against me with a lying tongue,
3 and with words of hatred they have encompassed me; and they fight against me without a cause.
4 For my love they are my adversaries*; but I [give] myself to prayer.
5 And they have rewarded me evil for good, and hatred for my love.
6 Set a wicked [man] over him, and let [the] adversary* stand at his right hand;
7 when he shall be judged, let him go out guilty, and let his prayer become sin~;
8 let his days be few, let another take his office;
9 let his sons be fatherless and his wife a widow;
10 let his sons be vagabonds and beg, and let them seek [their bread] far from their desolate places^;
11 let the usurer cast the net over all that he has, and let strangers despoil his labour;
12 let there be none to extend kindness+ to him, neither let there be any to favour his fatherless children;
13 let his posterity be cut off; in the generation following let their name be blotted out:
14 let the iniquity of his fathers be remembered with Jehovah, and may the sin of his mother not be blotted out;
15 let them be before Jehovah continually that he may cut off the memory of them from the earth:
16 because he did not remember to show kindness, but persecuted the afflicted and needy man, and the broken in heart, to slay him.
17 And he loved cursing; so let it come to him. And he did not delight in blessing; and let it be far from him.
18 And he clothed^^ himself with cursing like his vestment; so let it come into his bowels like water and like oil into his bones;

---

* *Satan* as in 1 Chronicles 21 v1 without the article. The same word in verses 4,20, 29 and Psalms 38 v20 and 71 v13

~ i.e. be imputed as sin

^ or 'ruins', see Psalm 102 v6. 'waste' in Leviticus 26 v31,33

+ or 'continue mercy'   ^^ or 'and let him clothe'

19 let it be to him as a garment with which he covers himself, and for a girdle with which he is constantly girded.
20 Let this be the reward** of my adversaries from Jehovah, and of them that speak evil against my soul.
21 But act for me, Jehovah, Lord, for your name's sake; because your loving-kindness is good, deliver me:
22 for I am afflicted and needy, and my heart is wounded within me.
23 I am gone like a shadow when it lengthens: I am tossed about like a locust;
24 my knees are failing through fasting, and my flesh has lost its fatness;
25 and I have become a reproach to them; [when] they look upon me, they shake their heads.
26 Help me, Jehovah my God; save me according to your loving-kindness:
27 that they may know that this is your hand; that you, Jehovah, have done it.
28 Let them curse, but [may] you bless; when they rise up, let them be ashamed, and let your servant rejoice.
29 Let my adversaries be clothed with confusion, and let them cover themselves with their shame as with a mantle.
30 I will greatly celebrate~~ Jehovah with my mouth; yes, I will praise him among the multititude.
31 For he stands at the right hand of the needy to save him from those that judge his soul.

** Literally 'the [work] wrought', 'wages'   ~~ or 'thank'

Psalm 110
A psalm of David

1 Jehovah said* to my Lord, "Sit at my right hand, until I put your enemies [as] footstool of your feet".
2 Jehovah shall send the sceptre of your might out of Zion: rule in the midst of your enemies.
3 Your people shall be willing~ in the day of your power^, in holy splendour: from the womb of the morning the dew of your youth [shall come] to you.
4 Jehovah has sworn and will not repent, you are priest for ever after the order of Melchisedek.
5 The Lord at your right hand will smite through kings in the day of his anger.
6 He shall judge among the nations; he shall fill [all places] with dead bodies; he shall smite through the head over a great country.
7 He shall drink of the brook in the way; therefore he shall lift up the head.

* as Genesis 22 v16, see also Psalm 36 v1
~ or 'voluntary offerings' 'shall offer themselves willingly'   ^ or 'forces (army)'

Psalm 111*

1 Hallelujah! I will celebrate Jehovah with [my] whole heart, in the council of the upright, and in the assembly.
2 Great are the works of Jehovah; sought out of all that delight in them.
3 His work is majesty and splendour, and his righteousness abides for ever.
4 He has made his wonders to be remembered~: Jehovah is gracious and merciful.
5 He has given meat to them that fear him; he is ever mindful of his covenant.
6 He has shown his people the power of his works, to give them the heritage of the nations.
7 The works of his hands are truth and judgment^; all his precepts are faithful:
8 maintained for ever and ever, done in truth and righteousness.
9 He sent deliverance+ for his people; he has commanded his covenant for ever: holy and terrible is his name.
10 The fear of Jehovah is the beginning of wisdom; a good understanding have all they that do [his precepts]: his praise abides for ever.

* An acrostic psalm: the letter of each half-verse follows the alphabetical order
~ or 'he has established a memorial of his wonderful works'   ^ or 'justice'+ or 'redemption'

Psalm 112*

1 Hallelujah! Blessed is the man that fears Jehovah, that delights greatly in his commandments.
2 His seed shall be mighty in the land~; the generation of the upright shall be blessed.
3 wealth and riches [shall be] in his house; and his righteousness abides for ever.
4 To the upright there arises light in the darkness; he is gracious and merciful and righteous.
5 It is well with the man that is^ gracious and lends; he will sustain his cause in judgment+.
6 For he shall not be moved for ever: the righteous shall be in everlasting remembrance.
7 He shall not be afraid of evil tidings; his heart is fixed confiding in Jehovah;
8 his heart is maintained, he is not afraid, until he see [his desire] upon his oppressors.
9 He scatters abroad, he gives to the needy; his righteousness abides for ever: his horn shall be exalted with honour.
10 The wicked [man] shall see [it] and be vexed; he shall gnash with his teeth, and melt away: the desire of the wicked shall perish.

* an acrostic psalm like Psalm 111   ~ or 'earth'   ^ or 'a good man is'
+ or 'he will carry on his affairs with right judgment'

Psalm 113

1 Hallelujah! Praise, you servants of Jehovah, praise the name of Jehovah.
2 Blessed be the name of Jehovah from this time forth and for evermore*.
3 From the rising of the sun to the going down of the same, let Jehovah's name be praised.
4 Jehovah is high above all nations, his glory above the heavens.
5 Who is like Jehovah our God, who has placed his dwelling on high;
6 who humbles himself to look on the heavens and on the earth?
7 He raises up the poor out of the dust; from the dung-hill he lifts up the needy,
8 to set [him] among nobles, among the nobles of his people.
9 He makes the barren woman to keep house [as] a joyful mother of sons. Hallelujah!

* in 1 Chronicles 16 v36 (cross-refd to Daniel 2 v20) phrase 'from eternity to eternity' is used

Psalm 114

1 When Israel went out of Egypt, the house of Jacob from a people of strange language,
2 Judah was his sanctuary, Israel his dominion.
3 The sea saw it and fled, the Jordan turned back;
4 the mountains skipped like rams, the hills like lambs.
5 What ailed you, sea, that you fled? Jordan, that you turned back?
6 You mountains, that you skipped like rams? You hills, like lambs?
7 Tremble, earth, at the presence of the Lord, at the presence of the God of Jacob,
8 who turned the rock into a pool of water, the flint into a fountain of waters.

Psalm 115

1 Not to us, o Jehovah, not to us, but to your name give glory, for your loving-kindness and for your truth's sake.
2 Why should the nations say, "Where then is their God?"
3 But our God is in the heavens; he has done whatsoever he pleased.
4 Their idols are silver and gold, the work of men's hands;
5 they have a mouth and don't speak; they have eyes and don't see;
6 they have ears and don't hear; a nose they have and they don't smell;
7 they have hands and they don't handle; they have feet and they don't walk; they don't give sound through their throat.
8 They that make them are like them – every one that confides in them.
9 O Israel, confide in Jehovah: he is their help and their shield.
10 House of Aaron, confide in Jehovah: he is their help and their shield.
11 You that fear Jehovah, confide in Jehovah: he is their help and their shield.
12 Jehovah has been mindful of us: he will bless, he will bless the house of Israel; he will bless the house of Aaron;
13 he will bless them that fear Jehovah, both the small and the great.
14 Jehovah will add to you more, to you and to your children.
15 You are blessed of Jehovah, who made the heavens and the earth.
16 The heavens are the heavens of Jehovah, but the earth he has given to the children of men.
17 The dead do not praise Jah, neither any that go down into silence;
18 but we will bless Jah from this time forth and for evermore*. Hallelujah!

---

* See note for Psalm 113 v2, i.e. 'from eternity to eternity'

Psalm 116

1 I love Jehovah, for he has heard my voice [and] my supplications;
2 for he has inclined his ear to me, and I will call upon him during [all] my days.
3 The bands* of death encompassed me, and the anguish~ of Sheol took hold of ^ me; I found trouble and sorrow:
4 then I called upon the name of Jehovah: "I beseech you, Jehovah, deliver my soul".
5 Gracious is Jehovah and righteous; and our God is merciful.
6 Jehovah keeps the simple: I was brought low and he saved me.
7 Return to your rest, o my soul, for Jehovah has dealt bountifully with you.
8 For you have delivered my soul from death, my eyes from tears, my feet from falling.
9 I will walk before Jehovah in the land+ of the living.
10 I believed, therefore I have spoken. As for me, I was greatly afflicted.
11 I said in my haste^^, "All men** are liars".
12 What shall I render to Jehovah [for] all his benefits toward me?
13 I will take the cup of salvation~~ and call upon the name of Jehovah.
14 I will perform my vows to Jehovah, yes, before all his people.
15 Precious in the sight of Jehovah is the death of his saints *(chasid)*.
16 Yes, Jehovah! For I am your servant, the son of your handmaid: you have loosed all my bonds.
17 I will offer++ to you the sacrifice of thanksgiving, and will call upon the name of Jehovah.
18 I will perform my vows to Jehovah, yes, before all his people,
19 in the courts of Jehovah's house, in the midst of you, o Jerusalem. Hallelujah!

* As Psalm 18 v4,5   ~ Literally 'anguishes' 'distresses'   ^ or 'found'
+ Literally 'lands'   ^^ or 'agitation' see Psalm 31 v22
** *The Adam* see Genesis 1 v27   ~~ Literally 'salvations' see Psalm 53 v6++
Literally 'sacrifice' as in Psalms 50 v14, 107 v22 etc

Psalm 117

1 Praise Jehovah, all you nations; laud him, all you peoples;
2 for his loving-kindness is great* toward us, and the truth of Jehovah [endures] for ever. Hallelujah!

* or 'is powerful', Literally 'it has prevailed' – see Psalm 103 v1

Psalm 118

1 Give thanks to Jehovah; for he is good; for his loving-kindness [endures] for ever*.
2 Oh let Israel say, that his loving-kindness [endures] for ever.
3 Oh let the house of Aaron say, that his loving-kindness [endures] for ever.
4 Oh let them that fear Jehovah say, that his loving-kindness [endures] for ever.
5 I called upon Jah in distress; Jah answered me [and set me] in a large place.
6 Jehovah is for me, I will not fear; what can man do to me?
7 Jehovah is for me among them that help me; and I shall see [my desire] upon them that hate me.
8 It is better to trust in Jehovah than to put confidence in man;
9 it is better to trust in Jehovah than to put confidence in nobles.
10 All nations encompassed me; but in the name of Jehovah I have destroyed them~.
11 They encompassed me, yes, encompassed me; but in the name of Jehovah I have destroyed them.
12 They encompassed me like bees; they have been quenched as the fire of thorns: for in the name of Jehovah I have destroyed them.
13 You have thrust hard at me that I might fall; but Jehovah helped me.
14 My strength and my song is Jah, and he has become my salvation^.
15 The voice of triumph and salvation is in the tents of the righteous: the right hand of Jehovah does valiantly;
16 the right hand of Jehovah is exalted, the right hand of Jehovah does valiantly.
17 I shall not die but live and declare the works of Jah.
18 Jah has chastened me sore; but he has not given me over to death.
19 Open to me the gates of righteousness: I will enter into them; I will praise+ Jah.
20 This is the gate of Jehovah: the righeous shall enter therein.
21 I will give you thanks for you have answered me and have become my salvation.

---

* verses 1-4 adopt similar style to Psalm 115 v9-13   ~ or 'mowed them down'
^ see Exodus 15 v2 ("My strength and my song is Jah')   + or 'give thanks'

22 [The] stone which the builders rejected has become the head of the corner^^;
23 this is of Jehovah; it is wonderful in our eyes.
24 This is the day that Jehovah has made; we will rejoice and be glad in it.
25 Oh save, Jehovah, I beseech you; Jehovah, I beseech you, oh send prosperity!
26 Blessed be he that comes in the name of Jehovah. We have blessed** you out of the house of Jehovah.
27 Jehovah is God, and he has given us light: bind the sacrifice~~ with cords – up to the horns of the altar.
28 You are my God and I will give you thanks; my God, I will exalt you.
29 Give thanks to Jehovah; for he is good; for his loving-kindness [endures] for ever.

^^ i.e. the cornerstone   ** or 'we bless'   ~~ strictly 'feast'

Psalm 119*

ALEPH
1 Blessed are the perfect in the way, who walk in the law of Jehovah.
2 Blessed are they that observe his testimonies, that seek him with the whole heart;
3 who also do no unrighteousness: they walk in his ways.
4 You have enjoined your precepts, to be kept diligently.
5 Oh that my ways were directed to keep your statutes.
6 Then I shall not be ashamed when I have respect to all your commandments.
7 I will give you thanks~ with uprightness of heart, when I shall have learned your righteous judgments.
8 I will keep your statutes; do not utterly forsake me.

* See Introduction   ~ or 'I will praise you'

BETH
9 Wherewithal shall a young man cleanse his path? By taking heed according to your word.
10 With my whole heart I have sought you: do not let me wander from your commandments.
11 Your word *(imrah)* I have hidden in my heart that I might not sin against you.
12 Blessed are you, Jehovah! Teach me your statutes.
13 With my lips I have declared all the judgments of your mouth.
14 I have rejoiced in the way of your testimonies as [much as] in all wealth.
15 I will meditate upon your precepts and have respect to your paths.
16 I delight myself in your statutes; I will not forget your word.

GIMEL
17 Deal bountifully with your servant [and] I shall live; and I will keep your word.
18 Open my eyes and I shall behold wondrous things out of your law.
19 I am a stranger in the land^; do not hide your commandments from me.
20 My soul breaks for longing after your judgments at all times.
21 You have rebuked+ the proud [that are] cursed, who wander from your commandments.

^ or 'on the earth'   + or 'you rebuke'

22 Roll off from me reproach and contempt; for I observe your testimonies.
23 Princes also did sit [and] talk together against me: your servant meditates in your statutes.
24 Your testimonies are also my delight [and] my counsellors.

DALETH
25 My soul cleaves to the dust: quicken^^ me according to your word.
26 I have declared my ways and you have answered me: teach me your statutes.
27 Make me understand the way of your precepts, and I will meditate upon your wondrous works.
28 My soul melts for sadness: strengthen me~~ according to your word.
29 Remove from me the way of falsehood and graciously grant me your law.
30 I have chosen the way of faithfulness; your judgments I have set [before me].
31 I cleave to your testimonies; Jehovah, do not let me be ashamed.
32 I will run the way of your commandments when you shall enlarge my heart.

^^ the word has a double sense, can mean 'making to live' and 'keeping alive'
~~ others translate 'raise me up'

HE
33 Teach me, o Jehovah, the way of your statutes and I will observe it [to] the end.
34 Give me understanding and I will observe your law; and I will keep it with [my] whole heart.
35 Make me walk in the path of your commandments for therein I do delight.
36 Incline my heart to your testimonies and not to gain.
37 Turn away my eyes from beholding vanity; quicken my in your way.
38 Establish your word *(imrah)* to your servant, who is [devoted] to your fear.
39 Turn away my reproach which I fear; for your judgments are good.
40 Behold, I have longed after your precepts: quicken me in your righteousness.

VAU

41 And let your loving-kindness come to me, o Jehovah - your salvation according to your word *(imrah)*.
42 So shall I have something with which to answer him that reproaches me; for I confide in your word.
43 And do not take the word of truth utterly out of my mouth; because I have hoped** in your judgments.
44 Then I will keep your law continually for ever and ever;
45 and I will walk at liberty++ for I have sought your precepts.;
46 and I will speak of your testimonies before kings and will not be ashamed;
47 and I will delight myself in your commandments which I have loved;
48 and I will lift up my hands to your commandments which I have loved, and I will meditate in your statutes.

** means 'to wait with earnest desire and longing' (see Psalm 69 v3), also in verses 49,74,81,114,147 and Psalm 147 v11
++ Literally 'at large' see Psalm 118 v5

ZAIN

49 Remember the word for your servant upon which you have caused me to hope.
50 This is my comfort in my affliction; for 1 your word *(imrah)* has quickened me.
51 The proud have derided me beyond measure: I have not declined from your law.
52 I remembered your judgments of old, o Jehovah, and have comforted myself.
53 Burning indignation has taken hold of me because of the wicked who forsake your law.
54 Your statutes have been my songs in the house of my pilgrimage.
55 I have remembered your name, o Jehovah, in the night, and have kept your law.
56 This I have had because I have observed your precepts.

1 or 'that'

CHETH

57 My portion, o Jehovah, I have said, is to keep your words 2.
58 I have sought your favour with my whole heart: be gracious to me according to your word *(imrah)*.
59 I have thought on my ways and turned my feet to your

2 or 'Jehovah is my portion: I have said that I will keep your words'

60 I have made haste and not delayed to keep your commandments.
61 The bands of the wicked have wrapped me round: I have not forgotten your law.
62 At midnight I rise up to give thanks to you because of your righteous judgments.
63 I am the companion of all that fear you and of them that keep your precepts.
64 The earth, o Jehovah, is full of your loving-kindness: teach me your statutes.

TETH
65 You have dealt well with your servant, o Jehovah, according to your word.
66 Teach me good discernment and knowledge for I have believed 3 in your commandments.
67 Before I was afflicted I went astray, but now I keep your word *(imrah)*.
68 You are good and do good; teach me your statutes.
69 The proud have forged falsehood against me: I will observe your precepts with [my] whole heart.
70 Their heart is as fat as grease: as for me 4, I delight in your law.
71 It is good for me that I have been afflicted that I might learn your statutes.
72 The law of your mouth is better to me than thousands of [pieces of] gold and silver.

3 or 'I believe'   4 see verses 78 and 87

YOD
73 Your hands have made me and fashioned me: give me understanding and I will learn your commandments.
74 They that fear you will see me and rejoice; because I have hoped in your word.
75 I know, Jehovah, that your judgments are righteousness and that in faithfulness you have afflicted me.
76 Oh let your loving-kindness be for my comfort, according to your word *(imrah)* to your servant.
77 Let your tender mercies come to me that I may live; for your law is my delight.
78 Let the proud be ashamed for they have acted perversely towards 5 me with falsehood: as for me, I meditate in your precepts.

5 or 'have subverted' see Psalm 146 v9

79 Let those that fear you turn to me, and those that know your testimonies.
80 Let my heart be perfect in your statutes so that I am not ashamed.

CAPH
81 My soul faints for your salvation; I hope in your word.
82 My eyes fail for your word *(imrah)*, saying, "When will you comfort me?"
83 For I have become like a bottle 6 in the smoke; I do not forget your statutes.
84 How many shall be the days of your servant? When will you execute judgment on them that persecute me?
85 The proud have dug pits for me which is not 7 according to your law.
86 All your commandments are faithfulness. They persecute me wrongfully: help me.
87 They had almost consumed me upon the earth; but as for me, I did not forsake your precepts.
88 Quicken me according to your loving-kindness, and I will keep the testimony of your mouth.

6 a leathern bottle   7 or 'who are not'

LAMED
89 For ever, o Jehovah, your word is settled in the heavens.
90 Your faithfulness is from generation to generation: you have established the earth and it stands.
91 By your ordinances they stand this day; for all things 8 are your servants.
92 Unless your law had been my delight, I should then have perished in my affliction.
93 I will never forget your precepts for by them you have quickened me.
94 I am yours, save me; for I have sought your precepts.
95 The wicked have waited for me to destroy me [but] I attend to your testimonies.
96 I have seen an end of all perfection: your commandment is exceeding broad.

8 strictly 'all' 'the whole'

MEM

97 Oh how I love your law! It is my meditation all the day.
98 Your commandments make me wiser 9 than my enemies for 9 or 'You make me wiser [through] your commandments...'
they are ever with me 10.
99 I have more understanding than all my teachers for your testimonies are my meditation.
100 I understand more than the aged because I have observed your precepts.
101 I have refrained my feet from every evil path that I might keep your word.
102 I have not departed from your judgments for it is you that has taught me.
103 How sweet are your words *(imrah)* to my taste! More than honey to my mouth!
104 From your precepts I get understanding; therefore I hate every false path.

10 or 'for it is mine'

NUN

105 Your word is a lamp to my feet and a light to my path.
106 I have sworn, and I will perform it, that I will keep your judgments.
107 I am afflicted very much; o Jehovah, quicken me according to your word.
108 Accept, I beseech you, Jehovah, the voluntary-offerings of my mouth, and teach me your judgments.
109 My life is continually in my hand but I do not forget your law.
110 The wicked have laid a snare for me, but I have not wandered from your precepts.
111 Your testimonies I have taken as a heritage for ever, for they are the rejoicing of my heart.
112 I have inclined my heart to perform your statutes for ever, to the end.

SAMECH

113 The double-minded I have hated, but your law I love.
114 You are my hiding-place and my shield: I hope in your word.
115 Depart from me, you evildoers and I will observe the commandments of my God.
116 Uphold me according to your word *(imrah)* that I may live; and don't let me be ashamed of my hope.
117 Hold me up and I shall be safe; and I will have respect to your statutes continually.

118 You have set at nought all them that wander from your statutes, for their deceit is falsehood.
119 You put away all the wicked of the earth 11 [like] dross; therefore I love your testimonies.
120 My flesh shudders for fear of you, and I am afraid of your judgments.

11 or 'land'

AIN
121 I have done judgment and justice: do not leave me to my oppressors.
122 Be surety for your servant for good; don't let the proud oppress me.
123 My eyes fail for your salvation, and for the word *(imrah)* of your righteousness.
124 Deal with your servant according to your loving-kindness and teach me your statutes.
125 I am your servant; give me understanding that I may know your testimonies.
126 It is time for Jehovah to work 12 : they have made your law void.
127 Therefore I love your commandments above gold, yes, above fine gold.
128 Therefore I regard all [your] precepts concerning all things to be right: I hate every false path.

12 or 'to act' – see Jeremiah 18 v23

PE
129 Your testimonies are wonderful, therefore my soul observes them.
130 The entrance of your words give light, giving understanding to the simple.
131 I opened my mouth wide and panted, for I longed for your commandments.
132 Turn to me 13 and be gracious to me, as you are wont to do to those that love your name.
133 Establish my steps in your word *(imrah)*, and do not let any iniquity 14 have dominion over me.
134 Deliver 15 me from the oppression of man, and I will keep your precepts.
135 Make your face shine upon your servant and teach me your

13 or 'look upon'   14 or 'vanity' 'inwardly devised evil' – see Psalm 55 v3
15 or 'ransom'

statutes.
136 My eyes run down with streams of water because they do not keep your law.

TZADE
137 You are righteous, Jehovah, and upright are 16 your judgments.
138 You have commanded your testimonies in righteousness and exceeding faithfulness.
139 My zeal destroys me because my oppressors *(tzar)* have forgotten your words.
140 Your word *(imrah)* is exceedingly pure 17 and your servant loves it.
141 I am little and despised: I have not forgotten your precepts.
142 Your righteousness is an everlasting righteousness 18, and your law is truth.
143 Trouble and anguish have taken hold upon me: your commandments are my delights.
144 Your righteousness of your testimonies is for ever: give me understanding and I shall live.

16 or 'and upright in' 17 or 'well refined' 'tried' see Psalm 18 v30
18 Literally 'a righteousness for ever' v144

KOPH
145 I have called with [my] whole heart; answer me, o Jehovah: I will observe your statutes.
146 I call upon you; save me and I will keep your testimonies.
147 I anticipate the morning-dawn and I cry: I hope in your word.
148 My eyes anticipate the night-watches that I may meditate in your word *(imrah)*.
149 Hear my voice according to your loving-kindness: o Jehovah, quicken me according to your judgment.
150 They have drawn close that follow after mischief: they are far from your law.
151 You, Jehovah, are near, and all your commandments are truth.
152 From your testimonies, I have known of old that you have founded them for ever.

RESH

153 See my affliction, and deliver me, for I have not forgotten [19] your law.

154 Plead my cause and redeem [20] me: quicken me according to your word *(imrah)*.

155 Salvation is far from the wicked, for they do not seek your statutes.

156 Many are your tender mercies, o Jehovah; quicken me according to your judgments.

157 Many are my persecutors and my oppressors *(tzar)*; I have not declined from your testimonies.

158 I beheld them that dealt treacherously and was grieved [21] because they did not keep your word *(imrah)*.

159 See how I have loved your precepts: quicken me, o Jehovah, according to your loving-kindness.

160 The sum of your word is truth, and every righteous judgment of yours is for ever.

19 or 'I do not forget'   20 see Psalm 103 v4
21 or 'and I loathed [them] see Psalm 139 v21

SHIN

161 Princes have persecuted me without a cause, but my heart stands in awe of your word.

162 I have joy in your word *(imrah)* as one that finds great spoil.

163 I hate and abhor falsehood; your law I love.

164 Seven times a day I praise you because of your righteous judgments.

165 Great peace have they that love your law and nothing stumbles them 22.

166 I have hoped for your salvation, o Jehovah, and have done your commandments.

167 My soul has kept your testimonies, and I love them exceedingly.

168 I have kept your precepts and your testimonies; for all my ways are before you.

22 or 'they have no stumbling-block'

TAU

169 Let my cry come near before you, Jehovah: give me understanding according to your word.

170 Let my supplication come before you: deliver me according to your word *(imrah)*.

171 My lips shall pour forth praise when you have taught me 23 your statutes.

172 My tongue shall speak aloud of 24 your word *(imrah)*, for all your commandments are righteousness.

173 Let your hand be for my help, for I have chosen your precepts.

174 I have longed for your salvation, o Jehovah, and your law is my delight.

175 Let my soul live and it shall praise you, and let your judgments help me.

176 I have gone astray like a lost sheep: seek your servant, for I have not forgotten your commandments.

23 or 'for you teach me' 24 or 'shall respond to' 'sing in answer to' – see Ezra 3v11

Psalm 120
A song of degrees*

1 In my trouble I called to Jehovah, and he answered me.
2 Jehovah, deliver my soul from the lying lip, from the deceitful tongue.
3 What shall be given to you, whall shall be added to you, you deceitful tongue?~
4 Sharp arrows of a mighty one, with burning coals of broom-wood.
5 Woe to me that I sojourn in Meshech, that I dwell among the tents of Kedar!
6 My soul has long dwelt with them that hate peace.
7 I [am for] peace; but when I speak, they [are] for war

* perhaps in the sense of 'going up'. See Psalm 122 v4. Others take it morally
~ or 'What shall the tongue of deceit give you, what shall it add to you?'

Psalm 121
A song of degrees

1 I lift up my eyes to the mountains: from where shall my help come?
2 My help [comes] from Jehovah who made the heavens and the earth.
3 He will not suffer your foot to be moved; he that keeps you will not slumber.
4 Behold, he that keeps Israel will neither slumber nor sleep.
5 Jehovah is your keeper, Jehovah is your shade upon your right hand;
6 the sun shall not smite* you by day nor the moon by night.
7 Jehovah will keep you from all evil; he will keep your soul.
8 Jehovah will keep your going out and your coming in from henceforth and for evermore.

* or 'beat upon'

Psalm 122
A song of degrees. Of David

1 I rejoiced when they said* to me, "Let us go into the house of Jehovah".
2 Our feet shall stand within your gates, o Jerusalem.
3 Jerusalem , which is built as a city that is compact together,
4 where the tribes go up, the tribes of Jah, a testimony~ to Israel, to give thanks to the name of Jehovah.
5 For there are set thrones for judgment, the thrones of the house of David.
6 Pray for the peace of Jerusalem: they shall prosper that love you.
7 Peace be within your bulwarks, prosperity^ within your palaces.
8 For my brethren and companions' sakes I will say, "Peace be within you!"
9 Because of the house of Jehovah our God I will seek your good.

*   or 'I rejoice in them that say'   ~ or 'Israel's custom'   ^ or 'restful security'

Psalm 124
A song of degrees. Of David

1 If it had not been Jehovah who was for us – oh let Israel say -
2 if it had not been Jehovah who was for us, when men rose up against us,
3 then they had swallowed us up alive when their anger was kindled against us;
4 then the waters had overwhelmed us, a torrent had gone over our soul;
5 then the proud waters had gone over our soul.
6 Blessed be Jehovah who did not give us up a prey to their teeth!
7 Our soul has escaped as a bird out of the snare of the fowlers: the snare is broken and we have escaped.
8 Our help is in the name of Jehovah, the maker of heavens and earth.

Psalm 125
A song of degrees

1 They that confide in Jehovah are as mount Zion which cannot be moved; it abides for ever.
2 Jerusalem! Mountains are round about her, and Jehovah is round about his people from henceforth and for evermore.
3 For the sceptre* of wickedness shall not rest upon the lot of the righteous in case the righteous put forth their hands to iniquity.
4 Do good, o Jehovah, to the good, and to them and that are upright in their hearts.
5 But as for such as turn aside to their crooked ways, Jehovah will lead them forth with the workers of iniquity. Peace~ be upon Israel!

*or 'rod'   ~ or 'shall be'

Psalm 126
A song of degrees

1 When Jehovah turned the captivity* of Zion, we were like them that dream.
2 Then was our mouth filled with laughter and our tongue with rejoicing: then they said among the nations^, Jehovah has done great things for them.
3 Jehovah has done great things for us [and] we are joyful.
4 Turn our captivity, o Jehovah, as the streams in the south+.
5 They that sow in tears shall reap with rejoicing:
6 he goes forth and weeps, bearing seed for scattering; he comes again with rejoicing, bearing his sheaves.

* Strictly 'the turning' or 'returning' in the sense of complete restoration and establishment of full blessing – see Psalm 14 v7   ^ *goim* a name given to the nations – Isaiah 1 v4
+ Hebrew *Negeb* i.e. the border land between the country later allotted to Judah and the wilderness

Psalm 127
A song of degrees. Of Solomon

1 Unless Jehovah builds the house, in vain do its builders labour in it; unless Jehovah keeps the city, the keeper watches in vain:
2 it is vain for you to rise up early, to lie down late, to eat the bread of sorrows*: so to his beloved one he gives sleep.
3 Lo, children are an inheritance from Jehovah, [and] the fruit of the womb a reward.
4 As arrows in the hand of a mighty man, so are children of youth.
5 Happy is the man *(geber)* that has filled his quiver with them. They shall not be ashamed when they speak with enemies in the gate.

* or 'labours' 'toils'

Psalm 128
A song of degrees

1 Blessed is every one that fears Jehovah, that walks in his ways.
2 For you shall eat the labour of your hands; you shall be happy and it shall be well with you.
3 Your wife shall be as a fruitful vine in the inner part of your house*; your children like olive-plants around your table.
4 Behold, thus shall the man *(geber)* be blessed that fears Jehovah.
5 Jehovah will bless you out of Zion; and may you see the good of Jerusalem all the days of your life,
6 and see your children's children. Peace be upon Israel!~

* or 'by the sides of your house'
~ or '...children's children [and] peace upon Israel'

Psalm 129
A song of degrees.

1 Many a time they have afflicted me from my youth – oh let Israel say -
2 many a time they have afflicted me from my youth; yet they have not prevailed against me.
3 The ploughers ploughed upon my back; they made their furrows long.
4 Jehovah is righteous: he has cut asunder the cords of the wicked.
5 Let them be ashamed and turn backward, all that hate Zion;
6 let them be as the grass upon the house-tops, which withers before it is plucked up,
7 with which the mower does not fill his hand, nor he that binds sheaves his bosom;
8 neither do the passers-by say, "The blessing of Jehovah be upon you; we bless you in the name of Jehovah!"

Psalm 130
A song of degrees.

1 Out of the depths I call upon you, Jehovah.
2 Lord, hear my voice; let your ears be attentive to the voice of my supplication.
3 If you, Jah, should mark iniquities, Lord, who shall stand?
4 But there is forgiveness with you that you may be feared.
5 I wait for Jehovah; my soul waits and in his word I hope*.
6 My soul [waits] for the Lord more than the watchers [wait] for the morning, [more than] the watchers for the morning~.
7 Let Israel hope in Jehovah, because with Jehovah there is loving-kindness and with him is plenteous redemption^;
8 and he will redeem+ Israel from all his iniquities

* as Psalms 38 v15, 119 v43, 130 v7, 131 v3   ~ or 'more than the watchers-for-the-morning watch for the morning'   ^ Lit 'ransom'

Psalm 131
A song of degrees. Of David

1 Jehovah, my heart is not haughty, nor my eyes lofty; neither do I exercise myself* in great matters and in things too wonderful for me.
2 Surely I have restrained and composed my soul like a weaned child with its mother: my soul within me is as a weaned child.
3 Let Israel hope in Jehovah from henceforth and for evermore.

* Literally "I have walked'

Psalm 132
A song of degrees

1 Jehovah, remember for David all his affliction;
2 how he swore to Jehovah, vowed to the Mighty One of Jacob:
3 I will not come into the tent of my house, I will not go up to the couch of my bed;
4 I will not give sleep to my eyes, slumber to my eyelids,
5 until I find out a place for Jehovah, habitations* for the Mighty One of Jacob...
6 Behold, we heard of it at Ephratah~, we found it in the fields of the wood^.
7 Let us go into his habitations*, let us worship at his footstool.
8 Arise, Jehovah, into your rest, you and the ark of your strength.
9 Let your priests be clothed with righteousness and let your saints *(chasid)* shout for joy.
10 For your servant David's sake, don't turn away the face of your anointed.
11 Jehovah has sworn [in] truth to David; he will not turn from it: "Of the fruit of your body I will set upon your throne;
12 "if your children keep my covenant and my testimonies which I will teach them, their children also for evermore shall sit upon your throne".
13 For Jehovah has chosen Zion; he has desired it for his dwelling:
14 "This is my rest for ever; here I will dwell, for I have desired it.
15 "I will abundantly bless her provision; I will satisfy her needy ones with bread;
16 "and I will clothe her priests with salvation, and her saints shall shout for joy.
17 "There I will cause the horn of David to bud forth+; I have ordained a lamp for my anointed.
18 "His enemies I will clothe with shame; but upon himself his crown^^ shall flourish".

* or 'tabernacles' see Psalm 84 v1   ~ Bethlehem-Judah
^ or 'of Jaar' used here poetically for Kirjath-jearim   + or 'sprout'   ^^ or 'diadem'

Psalm 133
A song of degrees. Of David

1 Behold, how good and how pleasant it is for brethren to dwell together in unity!
2 Like the precious oil upon the head, that ran down upon the beard, upon Aaron's beard, that ran down to the hem of his garments;
3 as the dew of Hermon that descends on the mountains of Zion; for there Jehovah has commanded the blessing, life for evermore*

* or perhaps 'the age' – see Psalm 28 v9

Psalm 134
A song of degrees.

1 Behold, bless Jehovah, all you servants of Jehovah, who by night* stand in the house of Jehovah.
2 Lift up your hands in the sanctuary~, and bless Jehovah.
3 Jehovah, the maker of heavens and earth, bless you out of Zion.

* Literally 'in the nights'   ~ or 'holiness' *kodesh* see Psalm 89 v5

•

Psalm 135

1 Hallelujah! Praise the name of Jehovah; praise, you servants of Jehovah,
2 you that stand in the house of Jehovah, in the courts of the house of our God.
3 Praise Jah; for Jehovah is good: sing psalms to his name; for it* is pleasant.
4 For Jah has chosen Jacob to himself, Israel for his own possession~.
5 For I know that Jehovah is great, and our Lord is above all gods.
6 Whatsoever Jehovah pleased, he has done in the heavens and on the earth, in the seas and all deeps;
7 who caused the vapours to ascend from the ends of the earth; who makes lightnings for the rain; who brings the wind out of his treasuries:
8 who smote the firstborn of Egypt, both of man and beast;
9 who sent signs and miracles into the midst of you, o Egypt, upon Pharaoh and upon all his servants;
10 who smote great nations and slew mighty kings,
11 Sihon king of the Amorites, and Og king of Bashan, and all the kingdoms of Canaan;
12 and gave their land for an inheritance to Israel his people.
13 Your name, o Jehovah, is for ever; your memorial^, o Jehovah, from generation to generation.
14 For Jehovah will judge+ his people, and will repent in favour of^^ his servants.
15 The idols of the nations are silver and gold, the work of men's hands:
16 they have a mouth and they don't speak; they have eyes and they don't see;
17 they have ears and they don't hear; neither is there any breath in their mouth.
18 They that make them are like them – every one that confides in them.
19 House of Israel, bless Jehovah; house of Aaron, bless Jehovah;
20 house of Levi, bless Jehovah; you that fear Jehovah, bless Jehovah.
21 Blessed be Jehovah out of Zion, who dwells at Jerusalem! Hallelujah!

* or 'this' – see Psalm 147 v1   ~ or 'peculiar treasure' – see Exodus 19 v5
^ see Exodus 3 v15   + or 'vindicate'
^^ see Deuteronomy 32 v36: or 'shall have compassion upon'

Psalm 136

1 Give thanks to Jehovah, for he is good; for his loving-kindness [endures] for ever:
2 give thanks to the God of gods, for his loving-kindness [endures] for ever;
3 give thanks to the Lord of lords, for his loving-kindness [endures] for ever.
4 To him who alone does great wonders, for his loving-kindness [endures] for ever:
5 to him that by understanding made the heavens, for his loving-kindness [endures] for ever;
6 to him that stretched out the earth above the waters, for his loving-kindness [endures] for ever;
7 to him that made great lights, for his loving-kindness [endures] for ever;
8 the sun for rule over* the day, for his loving-kindness [endures] for ever;
9 the moon and the stars for rule over* the night, for his loving-kindness [endures] for ever:
10 to him that smote Egypt in their firstborn, for his loving-kindness [endures] for ever,
11 and brought out Israel from among them, for his loving-kindness [endures] for ever,
12 with a powerful hand and with an outstretched arm, for his loving-kindness [endures] for ever;
13 to him that divided the Red Sea into parts, for his loving-kindness [endures] for ever,
14 and made Israel pass through the midst of it, for his loving-kindness [endures] for ever;
15 and overturned~ Pharaoh and his host in the Red Sea, for his loving-kindness [endures] for ever;
16 to him that led his people through the wilderness, for his loving-kindness [endures] for ever;
17 to him that smote great kings, for his loving-kindness [endures] for ever,
18 and slew famous kings, for his loving-kindness [endures] for ever;
19 Sihon king of the Amorites, for his loving-kindness [endures] for ever,

---

* or 'during'   ~ Literally 'shook out' or 'shot off' as Exodus 14 v27

20 and Og king of Bashan, for his loving-kindness [endures] for ever;
21 and gave their land for an inheritance, for his loving-kindness [endures] for ever:
22 an inheritance to Israel his servant, for his loving-kindness [endures] for ever:
23 who has remembered us in our low estate, for his loving-kindness [endures] for ever;
24 and has delivered^ us from our oppressors+, for his loving-kindness [endures] for ever:
25 who gives food to all flesh, for his loving-kindness [endures] for ever.
26 Give thanks to the God of the heavens: for his loving-kindness [endures] for ever.

^ Literally 'rent us from' as Psalm 7 v2   + or 'adversaries'

Psalm 137

1 By the rivers of Babylon, there we sat down; yes, we wept when we remembered Zion.
2 We hung our harps on the willows in the midst thereof.
3 For there they that carried us away captive required of us a song*; and they that made us wail~ [required] mirth, [saying], "Sing us [one] of the songs of Zion".
4 How should we sing a song of Jehovah's upon a foreign soil?
5 If I forget you, Jerusalem, let my right hand forget [its skill]:
6 if I do not remember you, let my tongue cleave to my palate: if I don't prefer Jerusalem above my chief joy.
7 Remember, o Jehovah, against the sons of Edom, the day of Jerusalem: who said, "Lay [it] bare, lay [it] bare down to its foundation!"
8 Daughter of Babylon, who is to be laid waste, happy is he that renders to you what you have meted out to us.
9 Happy is he that takes and dashes your little ones against the rock.

* Literally 'words of song'   ~ or 'our tormentors'

Psalm 138
[A psalm] of David

1 I will give you thanks with my whole heart; before the gods I will sing psalms of you.
2 I will bow down toward the temple of your holiness, and celebrate your name for your loving-kindness and for your truth; for you have magnified your word *(imrah)* above all your name.
3 In the day when I called you answered me; you encouraged me with strength* in my soul.
4 All the kings of the earth shall celebrate you, Jehovah, when they have heard the words *(omer)* of your mouth;
5 and they shall sing in~ the ways of Jehovah, for great is the glory of Jehovah.
6 For Jehovah is high; but he looks upon the lowly, and the proud he knows from afar.
7 Though I walk in the midst of trouble, you will revive me: you will stretch forth your hand against the anger of my enemies and your right hand shall save me.
8 Jehovah will perfect what concerns me: your loving-kindness, o Jehovah, [endures] for ever; do not forsake the works of your own hands.

* or 'mightily'   ~ or 'of'

Psalm 139

To the chief Musician. A psalm of David

1 Jehovah, you have searched me and known [me].
2 You know my sitting down and my rising up, you understand my thoughts from afar;
3 you search out* my path and my lying down, and are acquainted with all my ways;
4 for there is not yet~ a word on my tongue [but] lo, o Jehovah, you know it altogether.
5 You have beset me behind and before, and laid your hand upon me.
6 O knowledge too wonderful for me! It is high, I cannot [attain] to it.
7 Where shall I go from your spirit? And where flee from your presence?
8 If I ascend up to the heavens you are there; or if I make my bed in Sheol, behold, you [are there];
9 [if] I take the wings of the dawn [and] dwell in the uttermost parts of the sea,
10 even there your hand shall lead me, and your right hand shall hold me.
11 And if I say, "Surely darkness shall cover me, and the light about me be night";
12 even darkness does not hide from you, and the night shines as the day: the darkness is as the light.
13 For you have possessed my reins; you covered me^ in my mother's womb.
14 I will praise you, for I am fearfully, wonderfully made. Your works are marvellous; and [that] my soul knows full well.
15 My bones were+ not hidden from you when I was made in secret, curiously wrought in the lower parts of the earth.
16 Your eyes saw my unformed substance, and in your book all [my members] were written; [during many] days^^ they were fashioned when [as yet] there was none of them.
17 But how precious are your thoughts to me, o God! How great is the sum of them!
18 [If] I would count them, they are more in number than sand. When I awake, I am still with you.

---

* Literally 'sift'   ~ or 'even [before] there is' ^ or 'hedged in' – see Psalm 91 v4
+ or 'framework was'   ^^ or 'continuously'

19 Oh that you would slay the wicked, o God! And you men of blood, depart from me.

20 For they speak of you wickedly**, they take [your name] in vain, your enemies~~.

21 Do I not hate them, o Jehovah, that hate you? And do I not loathe them that rise up against you?

22 I hate them with perfect hatred; I account them my enemies.

23 Search me, o God, and know my heart; prove me, and know my thoughts 1;

24 and see if there is any grievous way 2 in me; and lead me in the everlasting way.

** or 'with evil intent'

~~ or '[They] who speak wickedly of you have lifted themselves up to lying – your enemies'

1 'anxious (or conflicting) thoughts' as Psalm 94 v19   2 or 'idolatrous way'

Psalm 140
To the chief Musician. A psalm of David

1 Free me, o Jehovah, from the evil man; preserve me from the violent man*:
2 who devise mischiefs in [their] heart; every day they are banded together for war.
3 They sharpen their tongues like a serpent; adders' poison is under their lips. Selah.
4 Keep me, o Jehovah, from the hands of the wicked [man], preserve me from the violent man, who devise to overthrow my steps.
5 The proud have hidden a snare for me and cords; they have spread a net by the wayside; they have set traps for me. Selah.
6 I have said to Jehovah, "You are my God: give ear, o Jehovah, to the voice of my supplications".
7 Jehovah, the Lord, is the strength of my salvation: you have covered my head in the day of battle~.
8 Do not grant the desire of the wicked, o Jehovah; do not further his device: they would exalt themselves. Selah.
9 [As for] the head of those that encompass me, let the mischief of their own lips cover them.
10 Let burning coals fall on them; let them be cast into the fire, into deep waters, so that they do not rise up again.
11 Do not let the man of [evil] tongue be established in the earth *(erets)*: evil shall hunt the man of violence to [his] ruin.
12 I know that Jehovah will maintain the cause of the afflicted one, the right of the needy.
13 Yes, the righteous shall give thanks to your name; the upright shall dwell in your presence.

* Literally 'man *(ish)* of violences, same in verse 4
~ or 'of arming for the battle'

Psalm 141
A psalm of David

1 Jehovah, I have called upon you: make haste to me; give ear to my voice when I call to you.
2 Let my prayer be set forth before you as incense, the lifting up of my hands as the evening oblation.
3 Set a watch, o Jehovah, before my mouth; keep the door of my lips.
4 Don't incline my heart to any evil thing, to practise deeds of wickedness with men that are workers of iniquity; and don't let me eat of their dainties.
5 Let the righteous smite me, it is kindness; and let him reprove me, it is an excellent oil which my head shall not refuse*: for yet my prayer also is [for them] in their calamities~.
6 When their judges are thrown down from the rocks, they shall hear my words, for they are sweet.
7 Our bones are scattered at the mouth of Sheol as when one cuts and cleaves [wood] upon the earth.
8 For my eyes are to you, Jehovah, Lord; in you do I trust: don't leave my soul destitute.
9 Keep me from the snare which they have laid for me, and from the traps of the workers of iniquity.
10 Let the wicked fall into their own nets whilst I pass over.

* or 'it is oil for the head; may my head not refuse it'
~ or 'is against their evil deeds'

Psalm 142
An instruction of David when he was in the cave: a prayer.

1 I cry to Jehovah with my voice: with my voice to Jehovah I make supplication.
2 I pour out my plaint before him; I show before him my trouble.
3 When my spirit was overwhelmed within me, then you knew my path. In the way wherein I have walked they have hidden a snare for me.
4 Look on my right hand and see; there is no man that knows me: refuge* has failed me; no man cares for my soul.
5 I cried to you, Jehovah: I said, "You are my refuge~, my portion in the land of the living".
6 Attend to my cry for I am brought very low; deliver me from my persecutors for they are stronger than me.
7 Bring my soul out of prison that I may celebrate^ your name. The righteous shall surround me because you deal bountifully with me.

* or 'a place of escape' as Psalm 59 v16 ~ or 'shelter'
^ or 'thank' , see also Psalm 138 v2

Psalm 143
A psalm of David

1 Jehovah, hear my prayer; give ear to my supplications: in your faithfulness answer me, in your righteousness.

2 And do not enter into judgment with your servant; for in your sight no man living shall be justified.

3 For the enemy persecutes my soul: he has crushed my life down to the earth; he has made me dwell in dark places as those that have been long dead.

4 And my spirit is overwhelmed within me; my heart within me is desolate.

5 I remember the days of old: I meditate on all your doing: I muse on the work of your hands.

6 I stretch forth my hands to you: my soul, as a parched land, [thirsts] after you. Selah.

7 Answer me speedily, o Jehovah; my spirit is failing: don't hide your face from me or I shall be like them that go down into the pit.

8 Cause me to hear your loving-kindness in the morning for in you I confide; make me know the way in which I should walk for to you I lift up my soul.

9 Deliver me, o Jehovah, from my enemies: to you I flee for refuge*.

10 Teach me to do your will~; for you are my God: let your good spirit lead me in a plain country^.

11 Revive me+, o Jehovah, for your name's sake; in your righteouness bring my soul out of trouble;

12 and in your loving-kindness cut off my enemies and destroy all them that oppress my soul: for I am your servant.

---

* as 'covered' in Isaiah 51 v16

~ or 'good pleasure' as in Psalms 103 v21, 40 v8

^ or 'land of uprightness'   + or 'keep me alive' as Psalm 119 v25

Psalm 144
[A psalm] of David

1 Blessed be Jehovah my rock who teaches my hands to war, my fingers to fight;
2 my mercy* and my fortress, my high tower and my deliverer, my shield and he in whom I trust, who subdues my people under me!
3 Jehovah, what is man *(Adam)* that you take knowledge of him, the son of man *(enosh)*~, that you take thought of him?
4 Man *(Adam)* is like vanity^; his days are as a shadow that passes away.
5 Jehovah, bow your heavens and come down; touch the mountains so that they smoke;
6 cast forth lightnings and scatter them; send forth your arrows and discomfit them:
7 stretch out your hands from above; rescue me and deliver me out of great waters, from the hand of aliens,
8 whose mouth speaks vanity and their right hand is a right hand of falsehood.
9 O God, I will sing a new song to you; with the ten-stringed lute I will sing psalms to you:
10 who gives salvation+ to kings; who rescues David from the hurtful sword.
11 Rescue me, and deliver me from the hand of aliens, whose mouth speaks vanity and their right hand is a right hand of falsehood.
12 That our sons may be as plants grown up in their youth; our daughters as corner-columns, sculptured after the fashion of a palace:
13 our granaries full, affording all manner of store; our sheep bringing forth thousands, ten thousands in our pastures;
14 our cattle laden [with young^^]; no breaking in and no going forth, and no outcry in our streets.
15 Blessed be the people that is in such a case! Blessed be the people whose God is Jehovah!

* see Psalm 59 v10: 'The God of my mercy'
~ Contrast here with Psalm 8 v4: here it is sinful man's fragility and impotence; there it is what God does in grace in exalting the 'Son of Man' (Adam)
^ or 'a breath' as Psalms 62 v9, 94 v11   + or 'victory'   ^^ or 'oxen well laden'

Psalm 145*

A psalm of praise. Of David

1 I will extol you, my God, o king, and I will bless your name for ever and ever.
2 Every day I will bless you, and I will praise your name for ever and ever.
3 Great is Jehovah and exceedingly to be praised; and his greatness is unsearchable.
4 One generation shall laud your works to another, and shall declare your mighty acts.
5 I will speak of the glorious splendour of your majesty and of your wondrous works.
6 And they shall tell of the might of your terrible acts; and your great deeds I will declare.
7 They shall abundantly utter~ the memory of your great goodness and shall sing aloud of your righteouness.
8 Jehovah is gracious and merciful; slow to anger and of great loving-kindness.
9 Jehovah is good to all; and his tender mercies are over all his works.
10 All your works shall bless you, Jehovah, and your saints^ shall bless you.
11 They shall tell of the glory of your kingdom and speak of your power;
12 to make known to the children of men his mighty acts, and the glorious splendour+ of his kingdom.
13 Your kingdom is a kingdom of all ages, and your dominion is throughout all generations^^.
14 Jehovah upholds all that fall, and raises up all that are bowed down.
15 The eyes of all wait upon you; and you give them their food in its season.
16 You open your hand and satisfy the desire of every living thing.
17 Jehovah is righteous in all his ways, and kind *(chasid)* in all his works.
18 Jehovah is near to all that call upon him, to all that call upon him in truth.

* An alphabetical psalm like Psalm 25 but the 14th letter is omitted
 ~ as in Psalm 19 v2   ^ or 'godly ones' as Psalm 30 v4
+ or 'the glory of the majesty'   ^^ literally 'in every generation and generation'

19 He fulfils the desire of them that fear him; he hears their cry and saves them.
20 Jehovah keeps all that love him, and all the wicked he will destroy.
21 My mouth shall speak the praise of Jehovah; and let all flesh bless** his holy name for ever and ever.

** or 'all flesh shall bless'

Psalm 146

1 Hallelujah! Praise Jehovah, o my soul.
2 As long as I live I will praise Jehovah; I will sing psalms to my God while I have my being.
3 Do not put confidence in nobles, in a son of man *(Adam)* in whom there is no salvation.
4 His breath goes forth, he returns to his earth; in that very day his purposes perish.
5 Blessed is he who has the God of Jacob for his help, whose hope is in Jehovah his God,
6 who made the heavens and the earth, the sea and all that is therein; who keeps truth for ever;
7 who executes judgment for the oppressed, who gives bread to the hungry.
8 Jehovah opens [the eyes of] the blind; Jehovah raises up them that are bowed down; Jehovah loves the righteous;
9 Jehovah preserves* the strangers; he lifts up~ the fatherless and the widow; but the way of the wicked he subverts.
10 Jehovah will reign for ever, [even] your God, o Zion, from generation to generation. Hallelujah!

* or 'keeps' see Psalm 145 v20
~ or 'upholds' as a witness in favour – see Deuteronomy 4 v26

Psalm 147

1 Praise Jah! For it is good. Sing psalms* of our God; for it is pleasant: praise is comely.
2 Jehovah builds up Jerusalem: he gathers the outcasts of Israel.
3 He heals the broken in heart, and binds up their wounds.
4 He counts the number of the stars; he gives names to them all.
5 Great is our Lord, and of great power: his understanding is infinite.
6 Jehovah lifts up the meek; he abases the wicked to the earth.
7 Sing to Jehovah with thanksgiving; sing psalms* upon the harp to our God:
8 who covers the heavens with clouds, who prepares rain for the earth, who makes grass grow upon the mountains;
9 who gives to the cattle their food, to the young ravens which cry.
10 He does not delight in the strength of the horse, he does not take pleasure in the legs of a man;
11 Jehovah takes pleasure in those that fear him, in those that hope in his loving-kindness.
12 Laud Jehovah, o Jerusalem; praise your God, o Zion.
13 For he has strengthened the bars of your gates; he has blessed your children within you;
14 he makes peace in your borders; he satisfies you with the finest of the wheat~.
15 He sends forth his oracles *(imrah)* to the earth: his word runs very swiftly.
16 He gives snow like wool, scatters the hoar frost like ashes;
17 he casts forth his ice like morsels: who can stand before his cold?
18 He sends his word, and melts them; he causes his wind to blow – the waters flow.
19 He shows his word to Jacob, his statutes and his judgments^ to Israel.
20 He has not dealt thus with any nation; and as for [his] judgments^, they have not known them. Hallelujah!

---

* see Psalms 30 v12, 47 v6, 138 v1   ~ Literally 'the fat of wheat'
^ or 'ordinances'

Psalm 148

1 Hallelujah! Praise Jehovah from the heavens; praise him in the heights.
2 Praise him, all his angels; praise him, all his hosts.
3 Praise him, sun and moon; praise him, all you stars of light.
4 Praise him, you heavens of heavens, and you waters that are above the heavens.
5 Let them praise the name of Jehovah, for he it is that commanded and they were created:
6 and he established them for ever and ever; he made [for them] a statute which shall not pass*.
7 Praise Jehovah from the earth, you sea-monsters and all deeps;
8 fire and hail, snow and vapour, stormy wind fulfilling his word;
9 mountains and all hills, fruit-trees and all cedars;
10 beasts and all cattle, creeping things and winged fowl;
11 kings of the earth and all peoples *(leummim)*, princes and all judges of the earth;
12 both young men and maidens, old men with youths -
13 let them praise the name of Jehovah: for his name alone is exalted; his majesty is above the earth and the heavens.
14 And he has lifted up the horn of his people *(ammim)*, the praise of all his saints~, [even] of the children of Israel, a people *(ammim)* near to him. Hallelujah!

* or 'which they do not transgress'   ~ or 'godly' *(chasid)*

Psalm 149

1 Hallelujah! Sing to Jehovah a new song; [sing] his praise in the congregation* of the godly *(chasid)*.
2 Let Israel rejoice in his Maker~; let the sons of Zion be joyful in their king.
3 Let them praise his name in the dance; let them sing psalms to him with the tambour and harp.
4 For Jehovah takes pleasure in his people *(leummim)*; he beautifies the meek with salvation.
5 Let the godly *(chasid)* exult in glory; let them shout for joy upon their beds.
6 Let the high praises of God be in their mouth^, and a two-edged sword in their hand:
7 to execute vengeance against the nations+, [and] punishment among the peoples *(leummim)*;
8 to bind the kings with chains, and their nobles with fetters of iron;
9 to execute upon them^^ the judgment written. All his saints *(chasid)* have this honour

* see Exodus 12 v6   ~ Hebrew word for 'Maker' is plural
^ Literally 'throat' per Psalm 5 v9
+ *Goim* a name given to the nations as Isaiah 1 v4.   ^^ or 'exercise among them'

Psalm 150

1 Hallelujah! Praise God in his sanctuary*; praise him in the firmament~ of his power.
2 Praise him in his mighty acts; praise him according to the abundance of his greatness.
3 Praise him with the sound of the trumpet; praise him with lute and harp;
4 praise him with the tambour and dance; praise him with stringed instruments and the pipe;
5 praise him with loud cymbals; praise him with high sounding cymbals.
6 Let everything that has breath praise Jah. Hallelujah!

* *kodesh* as Psalm 134 v2   ~ Literally 'the expanse'

Printed in Great Britain
by Amazon